ON BEING A CHRISTIAN

JOHN CAPPS IRWIN

ON BEING
A CHRISTIAN

HENRY M. BULLOCK, *General Editor*

ABINGDON PRESS • NEW YORK • NASHVILLE

ON BEING A CHRISTIAN

Copyright © MCMLVIII by Abingdon Press

SET UP, PRINTED, AND BOUND BY THE
PARTHENON PRESS, AT NASHVILLE,
TENNESSEE, UNITED STATES OF AMERICA

Contents

CHAPTER 1

On Being Religious

WHAT DOES IT MEAN TO BE A CHRISTIAN? AT FIRST GLANCE this seems to be a simple question, but only a little reflection reveals that it is not an easy one to answer. "Christian" is like other simple words we use daily—faith, hope, love. We know what we mean by them, but we would have difficulty defining them for others.

I

Part of the problem in stating what we mean by "Christian" is that we use the word to mean different things. FOR EXAMPLE, WE SOMETIMES SAY A PERSON IS A CHRISTIAN ONLY TO MEAN THAT HE IS A PRODUCT OF WESTERN CIVILIZATION RATHER THAN OF SOME NON-CHRISTIAN CULTURE. There is a sense in which our civilization has been so influenced by Christianity that even persons who are outside any formal religious life unconsciously follow Christian standards of conduct. However, it would certainly be unjustified to say that all Americans and western Europeans were Christians.

7

It is said that a shipwrecked sailor was once washed ashore on a South Pacific island. Seeing a campfire, he approached it cautiously, fearing to find cannibals dancing around a boiling pot. Instead he found a group of unshaven whites, drinking, swearing, and rolling dice. As he rushed to join them, he cried, "Thank heavens, I am among Christians!" To describe as "Christian" everyone not belonging to some other religion or culture is obviously an inadequate use of the word.

ANOTHER USE OF THE WORD "CHRISTIAN" IS TO DESCRIBE A GENEROUS, THOUGHTFUL PERSON. So deeply has the figure of Jesus impressed the world as one who lived with self-forgetfulness, gentleness, and concern for others that wherever we see these characteristics, we tend to identify them with him. Thus one dictionary definition of "Christian" is: a decent, civilized, or presentable person. However, all of us know persons who are generous to their families, kind to their neighbors, and self-giving in community service whose actions are in no way dictated by Christian considerations.

SOMETIMES WE USE "CHRISTIAN" TO IDENTIFY A PERSON WHO HOLDS MEMBERSHIP IN ONE OF THE CHURCHES. This is closer to the mark, but again not altogether accurate. Many church members joined in early youth and have since drifted away from any vital connection with their church. Others may participate in the life of the church out of habit or family loyalty but show little evidence that Christianity has influenced their lives in any noticeable degree. Still others may be sincere and faithful

8

without really understanding the mind and spirit of Jesus.

Henry Drummond, who was associated with Dwight L. Moody in his great evangelistic campaigns during the last century, used to tell of a cynic who said, "A Christian man is a man whose great aim in life is a selfish desire to save his own soul, who, in order to do that, goes regularly to church, and whose supreme hope is to get to heaven when he dies." Commenting on this, Mr. Drummond remarked that if there is anything a Christian is not, it is one who has a selfish desire to save his own soul. Church membership is not automatically a basis for identifying a Christian.

SOME WOULD INSIST THAT THE DESIGNATION "CHRISTIAN" SHOULD BE RESERVED FOR THOSE WHO BELIEVE THAT JESUS WAS THE SON OF GOD. Since Christians bear the name of Christ, it would seem logical that some high affirmation as to his nature would be expected of them. However, this alone is not enough. We are told in Scripture that "even the demons believe—and shudder" (James 2:19). Perhaps no word of Jesus causes us more searching self-examination than his warning to some who protested their devotion: "Not every one who says to me, 'Lord, Lord,' shall enter the kingdom of heaven" (Matthew 7:21). There is more to being a Christian than making a theological affirmation about the nature of Christ.

We see then that it is not so simple as we might suppose to answer the question, What does it mean to be a Christian? The difficulty is due, at least in part, to the fact that "Christian" is used in many senses and often not too accurately. As we seek for a more precise understanding of the word, we can at least agree that a Christian is a religious person. Let us then begin by asking, What does it mean to be religious?

II

We are forever dividing humanity into two parts. There are the tall and the short, the fat and the thin, the old and the young. There are also the religious and the irreligious. Think of some of the people you know. Is it not fairly easy to decide which ones are religious and which ones are not? What are some of the things that help you decide?

THE NONRELIGIOUS, OR SECULAR, PERSON ACTS AS IF THE WORLD WERE HIS OYSTER. He thinks that the world is made for him and that he is entitled to whatever he can lay his hands on. If he has good fortune, he assumes it is due to his cleverness, skill, and strength. He recognizes no divine Being or Power to which he owes any obligation. His own desires and purposes are his only law. He may be a pleasure seeker who makes "eat, drink, and be merry, for tomorrow we die" his rule, or he may be a hard-driving "go-getter" who seeks power and wealth. In any event, he has placed himself in the center of the world and is satisfied that he stands pretty tall.

THE RELIGIOUS PERSON, ON THE OTHER HAND, BELIEVES THAT "THE EARTH IS THE LORD'S, AND THE FULNESS THEREOF; THE WORLD, AND THEY THAT DWELL THEREIN." He senses a tremendous and mysterious Power all around him, and he bows himself in awe and reverence. This is why William Temple, the late great archbishop of Canterbury, said, "The heart of religion is not an opinion about God, such as philosophy might reach as the conclusion of its argument; it is a personal relation with God." The religious person has a serious attitude toward life and acts responsibly toward others. This does not mean that he is dour and stern. Indeed, he may well be the happiest of men, for personal good fortune is not necessary to his sense of significance.

THE SECULAR MAN IS PROUD AND ARROGANT; THE RELIGIOUS PERSON IS HUMBLE AND REVERENT. The irreligious man exploits every situation for his own advantage, while the religious man regards life as a trust. The one uses things and people; the other desires to be used. The first thinks the world owes him a living; the other believes he owes the world a life.

III

To be "religious," then, involves three things—a way of feeling, a way of thinking, and a way of acting. The emotions, the mind, and the will are involved in the life of religion.

FIRST OF ALL, THERE IS THE EMOTIONAL TONE—THE INDIVIDUAL'S BASIC FEELING ABOUT LIFE. This involves the attitudes which the person brings to every situation. We have seen that the central religious attitude is recognition that we are not our own. "It is [the Lord] that hath made us, and not we ourselves." Not only for the creation of our lives, but for the air that sustains us, the food that nourishes us, and the earth that houses us, we are dependent upon unseen forces outside ourselves. Particularly for all that makes us human—the life of mind and spirit, the heritage of former generations, the nurture of home and church, and the companionship of our fellows —are we the recipients of what theologians call "grace."

> Not as the owner,
> But as a guest you come, to fires not lit
> By hands of yours.[1]

Therefore, there is no room for pride and self-congratulation. Of myself I can do nothing—this is the classic confession of religion. This recognition of dependence is the basis for the warm feeling of gratitude and trust which marks the religious person.

BUT, SECOND, RELIGION ALSO INVOLVES A WAY OF THINKING. Religious persons have a "world view." What is the nature of the power or powers on which we are dependent? What is required of man? What must we do to establish right relations with "the Determiner of Destiny"? How do we explain the tragedy and limitation of life? What is the reward that men expect if they are obedient? What punishment is threatened if they offend? What will be the final outcome of our human adventure? Whatever the religion, the answers it has formulated to such questions as these constitute its theology, its way of thinking about life and the world.

---

[1] "When the Tree Bares" by Conrad Aiken. From *Collected Poems*. Oxford University Press. Copyright, 1921, 1949, by Conrad Aiken.

RELIGION, IN THE THIRD PLACE, ALSO CONSISTS OF A WAY OF ACTING. No matter what the faith, it presents its adherents with an expected standard of behavior, a code of ethics. This ideal of conduct will give practical guidance to the successful handling of the many relationships of daily life. It may prescribe in great detail the proper methods for preparing and eating food and the appropriate dress for various occasions. It will certainly guide the performance of duties in the family, the community, and the larger world. It will furnish the basis for decisions as to right and wrong, for both individuals and society. The "high" religions inspire conduct from their adherents which often goes far beyond the demands of law and custom.

A RELIGIOUS PERSON, THEN, IS ONE WHOSE WAYS OF FEELING, THINKING, AND ACTING ARE DETERMINED BY HIS AWARENESS OF DEPENDENCE UPON A POWER OR POWERS OUTSIDE HIMSELF. However, religious people are not necessarily Christian. Hindus, Buddhists, Moslems, and Jews are also religious. It is conceivable that people outside any of the recognized world religions might be basically religious in their approach to life. What more than being "religious" do we expect of Christians?

It is instructive in this connection to think of the rich young ruler (Matthew 19:16-22). Here was one who certainly met the tests of being religious. He took life seriously, he obeyed the moral law, he was conscientious in discharging the obligations of his faith. He was, nevertheless, conscious of something lacking. However, he turned away sorrowing from the radical commitment

13

demanded by Jesus. It is also helpful to think of the Pharisees. Sydney Cave suggests that in reading the New Testament "it is often well to substitute for Pharisees 'religious people,' for their sins were . . . sins to which all religious persons are tempted." [2] To be religious, then, is not enough. Something more is needful if we are to be truly Christian. Let us see if we can discover what this "something more" is.

FOR THOUGHT AND DISCUSSION

Read Matthew 19:16-22; Mark 10:17-22; Luke 18:18-23. On the basis of these passages make a list of the admirable traits which caused Jesus to "love" this young man. Do you think he was religious? Why?

On the basis of these three accounts what did the young man lack? Do these lacks throw any light on the difference between being religious and being Christian?

What is the evidence to support the view that we are dependent and of ourselves can do nothing? Do the people you know really believe this?

In what specific ways would we be changed if we really thought ourselves dependent upon God? (That is, what would it mean to believe that "in him we live, and move, and have our being"?) Is this what we mean by being religious?

Have you ever known any persons of another religious faith? In what ways were they more or less religious than the Christians you know? Are these differences important or superficial?

[2] *The Christian Way* (New York: Philosophical Library, Inc., 1949), page 50.

CHAPTER 2

On Being a Christian

THE CLUE TO WHAT IT MEANS TO BE A CHRISTIAN IS FOUND in the name itself—*Christ*-ian, that is, Christ's man; one belonging to Christ. This was not the first name by which the followers of Jesus were called. Earlier designations were "disciples," "saints," "those of the way." One writer[1] lists twelve titles by which the early Church was known, but the term which became definitive was this phrase which identifies the follower with his Lord.

We are told it was at Antioch that the disciples were first called Christians (Acts 11:26). This would have been ten or twelve years after the Crucifixion. Probably the name was applied by outsiders and very likely in derision. However, the name caught on because it unconsciously struck at the center. What makes Christians different is Christ. A Christian is one who belongs to Christ, one whose ways of feeling, thinking, and acting are determined by Christ.

---

[1] Dwight E. Stevenson, *Faith Takes a Name* (New York: Harper & Bros., 1954).

I

In an earlier discussion we saw that the central religious attitude is a feeling of dependence upon a Power or powers not ourselves. For the Christian this sense of dependence comes to a focus in Christ. That is why Christian faith from the earliest times has always spoken of Jesus Christ our *Lord*. That is why candidates for church membership are asked, "Do you confess Jesus Christ as your Savior and Lord?"

In Bible times the word "Lord" implied the relationship of master and slave or of political ruler and subject. In either case it was a relation between persons involving ultimate and total loyalty. "No man can serve two masters." When the Christian considers the circumstances of his life—how he has been surrounded with good influences, nurtured by home and church, and placed in situations beyond his strength which have driven him to God—he feels with the apostle Paul that he has been captured ("elected") by the divine initiative. When he contemplates Calvary and its cross, he, like the slave, feels that he has been "bought with a price." Yet his servitude is not one of compulsion, for he knows he has freely chosen his Master and has heard him say, "Henceforth I call you not servants; . . . but I have called you friends."

AGAIN, THE CHRISTIAN FEELS THAT HE IS A SUBJECT WHO MUST OBEY HIS SOVEREIGN. He has heard much of a Kingdom, and he is its citizen. The Kingdom has laws which he must obey. He has a cause and a Leader. The Church has often used the metaphor of military life to express its sense of unqualified devotion to its Lord: "Am I a soldier of the cross?" "Onward, Christian soldiers," "Like a mighty army moves the Church of God," and many more. The Christian has a Leader, but he has not been drafted; he has a Lord, but he has chosen his service. He has heard a gracious invitation, "Follow me," and has responded with glad obedience.

Thus a Christian is first of all one who has committed himself in loyalty to Christ as Lord of life. This warm, freely given personal loyalty to a Lord is the central core of the emotional, or feeling, side of Christian experience. Thus Dr. Douglas Horton said in his first convocation address as dean of the Harvard Divinity School: "The church is not a company of people who assent to an idea, . . . but a company of people grateful and loyal to a person in history, Jesus Christ." [2]

Loyalty to Christ as Lord sustained the early Christians in persecution and was the inspiration of saints and martyrs. It has led missionaries to the far places of the earth and has compelled others to devote themselves to the city's slums and to the neglected areas of the nation's life. Best of all, it has enabled common, everyday folks to reject the wrong and do the right, and to live lives of beauty, dignity, and peace. Such loyalty has been offered with no expectation of reward in terms of comfort, success, or convenience. *Loyal devotion to Christ our Lord will give our lives the direction and motive power they need.*

---

[2] *Christian Century* news report, November 16, 1955, page 1344.

II

HOWEVER, CHRISTIANITY IS MORE THAN A WAY OF FEELING ABOUT CHRIST AS LORD. IT IS A WAY OF THINKING ABOUT LIFE AND THE WORLD, AND THIS TOO IS DETERMINED BY CHRIST. Every man has his way of thinking about life— his world view. Either he will think that the world is an accident and that life has no meaning, or he will see the world as God's creation and life as having a purpose which can be known. Consciously or unconsciously, each one of us comes to view the world as a playground, a battlefield, a grab bag, or a trust.

When Christians think about the world and its meaning, they begin with what they know of Jesus and his teaching from the biblical records. They also have what previous generations have thought and their own fresh experience of what Paul called "the mind of Christ." From all this data they form their way of thinking about life. This is the task of Christian theology.

Past ages have formulated their beliefs in the great creeds of the Church. The early Church has left us the Apostles' and the Nicene creeds. The Reformation produced restatements in terms of the issues of that day, such as the Augsburg and the Westminster confessions and the thirty-nine articles of the Anglicans. Often the language of far-off controversies is hard for us to understand. Furthermore, the issues which make faith difficult and which demand clarification differ from age to age. Therefore, each generation has the task of formulating its faith in terms meaningful to its own times.[3] However, in spite of changing accents and language there is a basic body of belief—a Christian way of thinking about life—that runs through the ages.

It is the Christian faith:

—that the God who rules the universe is to be understood as Justice, and Mercy, and Love;

—that God has revealed and is revealing himself to man, and that it is man's highest joy to respond to this revelation which God is making of himself and his purposes;

—that the nature of God is perfectly revealed in Jesus Christ;

—that God requires of us lives of truth, goodness, and love;

—that God in Christ makes of us a new creation and empowers us through the Holy Spirit;

—that the ultimate triumph of righteousness, the rule of God, is certain;

—that human personality is the highest product of the universe and will triumph over physical death.

In the past it has been customary to emphasize the peculiar or unique emphasis made by each branch of Christendom until we have often lost sight of the fact that we all belong to one household of faith. However, the coming together of the great majority of Protestants

---

[3] Two "Affirmations of Faith" in contemporary language are provided for use in public worship in editions since 1939 of the *Methodist Hymnal*, page 512.

in the World Council of Churches has emphasized again that there is *a* Christian way of thinking. Thus the First Assembly of the World Council, meeting in Amsterdam, was able to say with all the weight of 151 member churches behind it:

> There is a word of God for our world. It is that the world is in the hands of the living God, Whose will for it is wholly good; that in Christ Jesus, His Incarnate Word, Who lived and died and rose from the dead, God has broken the power of evil once for all, and opened for everyone the gate into freedom and joy in the Holy Spirit; that the final judgment on all human history and on every human deed is the judgment of the merciful Christ; and that the end of history will be the triumph of His Kingdom, where alone we shall understand how much God has loved the world. This is God's unchanging word to the world.[4]

To be a Christian is to have a way of thinking about life inspired by Christ.

III

CHRISTIANITY IS ALSO A WAY OF ACTING. From the beginning it has been recognized that Christians lived differently from others. Jesus insisted that just as trees are known by their fruits, so a good life must of necessity

---

[4] *Man's Disorder and God's Design* (New York: Harper & Bros.), Book IV, page 232.

bring forth good fruit. "Why do you call me Lord, and not do what I tell you?" we hear him asking sadly at the close of Luke's version of the Sermon on the Mount (6:46 R.S.V.). Paul expected his converts to confront paganism with a quality of life in marked contrast to the selfish pleasure seeking which prevailed. They were to "put off the old nature with its practices and . . . put on the new nature" and "present [their] bodies as a living sacrifice, holy and acceptable to God" (R.S.V.).[5] Historians tell us that Christianity conquered the Roman world because the Christians obeyed the command of their Master to "love one another" so persuasively that they won first the admiration and then the adherence of their rivals. One suspects that a Christian life is still the best argument for Christianity!

THE CHRISTIAN WAY OF ACTING, AS THE CHRISTIAN WAY OF FEELING AND OF THINKING, IS DERIVED FROM CHRIST. In part Christians form their standards of conduct from the teaching of Jesus, such as the Sermon on the Mount and the parable of the last judgment. They also find guidance in the ethical passages of Paul's letters and of other New Testament writings. However, those who turn to the Gospels expecting to find a code of conduct covering all conceivable situations of modern life are bound to be disappointed. The Christian religion is not a set of rules to be obeyed; it is a life of fellowship with God in Christ.

---

[5] See Colossians 3:1–4:5 and Romans 12:1–15:13 for examples of Paul's characteristic way of closing his letters with ethical advice.

However, Christians find something better than rules of conduct in the New Testament. They find Christ himself. They read of his life of trustful obedience to the will of his heavenly Father. They see him responding to the needs of all sorts and conditions of men. They find him taking a towel and performing menial service that others were too proud to do. They hear him from the cross praying for those who despitefully used him. This is how Christians are to act—not in dogged obedience to rules, but in his Spirit and fellowship with him.

IV

WHAT DOES IT MEAN TO BE A CHRISTIAN? IT MEANS TO BE CHRIST'S MAN WITH FEELINGS, THOUGHTS, AND ACTIONS TRANSFORMED BY THIS ALLEGIANCE. It means a life lived under the direction of Christ as Lord. But note, it must be the entire life—emotions, mind, and will.

Most of the misunderstandings among Christians result from identifying Christianity with only one aspect of personality. For example, there are those who have had certain emotional experiences in connection with their Christian decision and who question the sincerity of those who have some other experience. This not only overlooks the fact of human differences but easily turns emotion into sentimentality. Others are impressed by the importance of correct belief and identify being Christian with the assent to certain verbal formulations. This produces the hard, unloving attitude which conducts heresy trials or separates creed from deed so that the workaday world is unredeemed. Still others want to lay down a strict code of behavior to which all Christians must conform. This easily leads to the same self-righteous pride which Jesus so forcefully condemned.

On the contrary, being a Christian will mean concern for others, love of our enemies, concern for the suffering of children, for the frustrations of youth, for the loneliness of the aged, for the emptiness of life of the sinful.

To be a Christian is to place every area of life under the sway of Christ. *It is nothing less than living the whole of life in fellowship with him.* What it may mean in detail to follow Jesus in various areas of life will be the subject of our inquiry in subsequent chapters of this study. It is enough to see now that if we are to be Christians, follow him we must. Fifty years ago as a brilliant young scholar Albert Schweitzer closed the first book that brought him fame, *The Quest of the Historical Jesus,* with these moving words:

> He comes to us as One unknown, without a name, as of old, by the lake-side. He came to those men who knew Him not. He speaks to us the same word: "Follow thou me!" and sets us to the tasks which He has to fulfil for our time. He commands. And to those who obey Him, whether they be wise or simple, He will reveal Himself in the toils, the conflicts, the sufferings which they shall pass through in His fellowship, and, as an ineffable mystery, they shall learn in their own experience Who He is.

FOR THOUGHT AND DISCUSSION

Read Mark 2:13-28. What conduct on the part of Jesus did the religious leaders of his time find it hard to understand? Why did this cause them difficulty? Do you think these leaders were sincere and earnest men? Why or why not? Does this conflict help you see that it is important how we think of our religion? Does it throw any light on the difference between being religious and being Christian? In what way?

Read the membership vows taken by persons who unite with your church. What do these questions indicate that it means to be a Christian?

In our society we no longer know the relation between master and slave. Can you think of some contemporary terms that imply a similar relation to that meant when the New Testament calls Jesus "Lord"?

What about the high-minded humanists who try to live according to the law of love in human relations without reference to God? Are such persons trying to live up to high ideals without laying hold on the source of power which is essential to such living? Do such persons fail to see that they are trying to be "good" under their own power and miss the fact that one can love his neighbor as himself only through the grace of God?

Does it make any difference what a person believes? Why? What do Christians believe? Study the three creedal statements provided for Methodist use (*Methodist Hymnal*, p. 512) or corresponding documents if you belong to another denomination. Do you see any important differences between them? How do they compare with the statement of the World Council of Churches quoted on page 20?

Will being a Christian have any effect upon a person's conduct? Why and how? Are Christians agreed on what Christian conduct is? Can you give some examples of specific areas where opinion differs? Can we say that persons are Christians only if they act in ways we think they should? Why or why not? What help can we get from the Bible in deciding how Christians should act?

Here are some statements by outstanding Christian leaders. Do any of them help you formulate what it means to you to be a Christian?

HENRY DRUMMOND: The Christian man is he who lives under the influence of Jesus Christ.

EDGAR S. BRIGHTMAN: The one vital essential to being a Christian is the desire to follow Jesus.

KIRBY PAGE: To live every day as a good member of God's home: this is the religion of Jesus.

TOYOHIKO KAGAWA: To imitate Jesus and follow in his footsteps—this is Christianity.

ANDREW W. BLACKWOOD, JR.: Christianity is a personal relationship with Christ. It is not primarily ideas about him, nor following rules and regulations, nor belonging to an organization, nor participating in the right ceremonies.

LESLIE WEATHERHEAD: There ought to be a time when the growing soul . . . accepts Christ's mastery and dedicates his life or her life to him.

CHAPTER 3

Being a Christian in Personal Life

"IF RELIGION DOES NOT BEGIN WITH THE INDIVIDUAL, IT never begins, and has no being." But if it "ends with the individual, it ends." So says Dr. George M. Buttrick, preacher to Harvard University.[1] This is a dramatic way of saying that the distinction we often make between personal and social Christianity is a purely academic one for purposes of discussion. *Actually the personal and the social aspects of religion are the two sides of a coin, the inside and outside of the cup, the upper and lower blades of the shears.* Apart from the other neither can perform the functions required of it. If an individual has any genuine personal religious commitment, it is bound to show in his social relationships.

However, sincere people continue to separate these two sides of the Christian life. To some, Christianity is purely a matter of individual relation to God in Christ.

[1] *Jesus Came Preaching* (New York: Chas. Scribner's Sons, 1931), page 115.

They ask their preachers to "stick to the simple gospel," and they do not understand why church bodies feel called upon to make pronouncements upon social and economic affairs. Others, who have been deeply stirred by the human cost of poverty, slums, unemployment, indulgence in use of alcoholic beverages, discrimination, prejudice, national and racial hatreds, and war, feel that the coming kingdom of God waits for a concerted attack by Christians upon the social evils of our times. Each of these groups feels that the other is in some way diluting or perverting "the religion of Jesus."

In pursuing our investigation of what it means to be a Christian, we shall keep both aspects of Christian faith in mind, looking first at the meaning of Christian commitment for personal life and then at its significance for social life. However, as we do so, we shall always remember that we are looking at only one side of an indivisible whole.

I

First of all, it may be helpful to look at some common misconceptions of what it means to be Christian in personal life. SOME HAVE FELT THAT ACCEPTING CHRIST REQUIRED THEM TO LEAD CARBON COPIES OF HIS LIFE. Thus the mendicant preachers of the Middle Ages left home and family and accepted vows of poverty and celibacy in an effort to live as Jesus lived. Doubtless even today many hold back from wholehearted Christian commitment because they assume this would require some ex-

treme, ascetic life or at least entering full-time professional Christian service. The effort to duplicate exactly
the life Jesus led deserves praise for taking Christian
decision seriously, but it overlooks several factors. It is
impossible to reproduce the conditions of life of one
century and country in another or to live in a cold
northern climate as one might in Palestine.[2] Further,
Jesus did not ask all who heard and accepted him in
his lifetime to follow him in the literal way the Twelve
did. Mary, Martha, and Lazarus continued to live in
Bethany; and the letters of Paul are full of allusions to
"saints" who did not leave home and occupation to
become traveling evangelists. We are called not to duplicate the external conditions of Jesus' life, but to translate
his spirit into the conditions of the twentieth century in
the place where we live, each according to his own gifts
and abilities.

AN EVEN MORE WIDELY HELD IDEA IS THAT TO BE A
CHRISTIAN IS TO FOLLOW CERTAIN RELIGIOUS AND MORAL
RULES WHICH WE WILL FIND IN THE BIBLE. Thus many
Christian sects have been formed around convictions as
to the proper day of the week for worship, the correct
mode of baptism, nonparticipation in war, or abstention
from such things as alcohol and tobacco. Early Methodists laid great stress upon abstaining from theater and
circus, dancing, card playing, and giving up costly ap-
parel. However, thoughtful Christians have come to see

---

[2] Most efforts to imitate Jesus literally result in an unconscious substitution of
the customs of their own century for those of the first. Thus strict Mennonite communities preserve the dress and customs of sixteenth-century middle Europe rather
than first-century Palestine.

that what they find in the Bible is not regulations but principles. We read, "Thou shalt not kill," but we are left to decide whether or not this forbids capital punishment and participation in war. We are told that the Sabbath was made for man, not man for the Sabbath, but what that leaves us free to do is not spelled out. For example, in Chicago public high schools schedule their athletic contests on Friday nights and Saturday afternoons, while Catholic schools play theirs on Sunday afternoons. We have to decide which practice is more in harmony with the principle Jesus announced.

Controversy as to whether loyalty to Christ involves obedience to a set of rules is as old as Christianity. The first church council was held over this matter (Acts 21:17-25), and the subject is argued at length in Paul's letter to the Galatians. Here we read Paul's conviction that we have been saved for freedom and liberty, not for slavish obedience to law (Galatians 5:1). Augustine put the matter daringly when he told his people to love God and do what they pleased. Of course he understood that utter and complete love of God would transform what people please to do!

The preceding generation was greatly helped in its effort to be Christian in personal life by a little book which had enormous circulation, *In His Steps* by Charles M. Sheldon. This told the story of a newspaperman whose life, and in turn his community, was radically changed when he began to ask in every situation he faced, "What would Jesus do?" This approach recognizes that Christians are expected to be different, while meeting the two difficulties we have previously faced, namely, that it is impossible to copy the terms of life in the first century and that we do not have specific rules of conduct in the Bible. *Asking what Jesus would do can be a helpful exercise if we will keep in mind that not all sincere Christians will answer the question the same way!* On some matters—the owning of slaves, for example—the Church has come to a common mind as to what Jesus would do, but on others there is continuing debate. Thus some ministers enter the military chaplaincy on the ground that Jesus would certainly go to men in need, and others refuse the chaplaincy on the basis that they cannot conceive of Jesus in uniform. So long as each group respects the sincerity and devotion of the other, the search for Christ's will in this area can fruitfully continue. *However, the expectation that every honest person will come to the same conclusion we have reached can lead only to self-righteousness and spiritual pride, the sins Jesus most scathingly rebuked.*

So far we have seen that it is not as simple and obvious as we might suppose to say what it means to be Christian in personal life. However, the difficulty must not prevent the effort. If Christianity is true, it is the most stupendous fact in the world, and no one could accept the Christian faith and not be radically changed. Gamaliel Bradford said of Daniel Webster, "I do not see the slightest evidence that religion ever took profound hold of him, either as a matter of agony or as a matter of rapture." Earnest Christians may well hope that their faith will mean to them both rapture and agony as they live with God in this imperfect world.

II

Perhaps it will help us to ask at this point what we mean by "personal religion." CHRISTIANS MEAN BY PERSONAL RELIGION A LIFE OF FELLOWSHIP WITH GOD IN CHRIST. The Christian ideal is that every moment is lived and every decision and action is taken consciously as a child of God. This continuous fellowship with God releases Christianity from its prison of one day a week and its confinement to certain "religious" practices; it takes religion out of the walls of the church and into the walks of life. This experience of conscious fellowship with God is Christian because it is Christ who makes it possible. It is he who has revealed God to us as a loving Father, and it is his life and death that have reconciled man to God and man to man.

It is in this life of fellowship with God that we are to imitate Jesus. In our one glimpse of Jesus as a lad we hear him say, "Did you not know that I must be in my Father's house?" (R.S.V.). From the cross he cries, "Father, into thy hands I commend my spirit." In between we find him seeking the Father's will for his life in the wilderness, showing the Father's purpose through teaching and healing, and observing long vigils of prayer that God's will, not his, might be done. To be a Christian in personal life is to have similar fellowship with God.

THE BREAKING OF CONSCIOUS FELLOWSHIP WITH GOD IS

WHAT WE MEAN BY SIN. Sin has been defined as "wrong-doing seen in its relation to God." [3] However, sin may involve wrong attitudes and thoughts as well as wrong actions. Indeed, sin is often seen in hidden motive and desire rather than in overt act. That is why the Sermon on the Mount demands a "higher morality" than obedience to human standards. The sin of murder does not lie in the physical violence, but in the hate that produces it; lust rather than the lustful act is the sin of adultery. So complex are our motives that often what seems right is really wrong. As one of our poets has said:

> The last temptation is the greatest treason:
> To do the right deed for the wrong reason. [4]

God, who looks on the heart, is not misled by the conventional respectability which cloaks most of our lives. He "unto whom all hearts are open, all desires known, and from whom no secrets are hid," knows us better than we know ourselves. That is why the classic Christian confession is, "All have sinned, and come short of the glory of God."

IT IS WHEN WE REALIZE OUR SEPARATION FROM GOD THAT CHRISTIANITY OFFERS US SALVATION. Paul called this experience "new life in Christ." "It is no longer I who live," he wrote, "but Christ who lives in me" (R.S.V.). Our old lives were organized around self-will, or the desire

---

[3] H. F. Rall, *Religion as Salvation* (Nashville: Abingdon Press, 1953), page 60.
[4] From *Murder in the Cathedral* by T. S. Eliot, copyright, 1935, by Harcourt, Brace and Company, Inc. and reprinted with their permission.

for social approval, or the search for wealth, prestige, or power. When Christ becomes the Lord of life, his will is placed at the center. William James defined conversion as

> the process, gradual or sudden, by which a self hitherto divided, and consciously wrong, inferior and unhappy, becomes unified and consciously right, superior and happy, in consequence of its firmer hold upon religious realities. . . . To say that a man is "converted" means . . . that religious ideas previously peripheral in his consciousness, now take a central place, and that religious aims form the habitual centre of his energy.[5]

Paul used the figure of death and resurrection. Our old nature is crucified with Christ; we go down into the grave with him. But a new nature, the Christian personality, arises, a continuing commentary upon the resurrection (see Romans 6:1-14).

PERSONAL RELIGION BEGINS FOR EACH CHRISTIAN WHEN HE HAS SUCH A FACE TO FACE INVOLVEMENT WITH GOD IN CHRIST. This experience does not come for all at the same time or in the same way. Some have a stormy, agonizing struggle with sin or doubt; others unfold quietly and gradually like an opening flower. Some come face to face with God in Christ as children, others as youths, still others as mature men and women. At any rate, at some point in life they have consciously known that only in Christ did their conflicting purposes and

---

[5] William James, *The Varieties of Religious Experience* (New York: Longmans, Green & Co., 1928), pages 189, 196.

desires come into focus, and only in fellowship with God did life make sense. Until we know what it is to organize our entire lives—our feeling, thinking, and acting—around the fact of God as he comes to us in Christ, we cannot know what is meant by personal Christian living.

III

If the good life is the religious life and if being Christian means a life of conscious fellowship with God, why do many of us find it difficult to maintain a sense of vitality in our personal religion? Dr. Harry Emerson Fosdick has well described the spiritual condition of multitudes, "The trouble with many of us is not that we think God untrue but that we find him unreal." [6] If God "is not far from each one of us, for 'in him we live and move and have our being,'" why does he so often seem unreal?

FOR ONE THING, IT IS BECAUSE WE SO OFTEN HAVE NO SENSE OF NEED. We saw earlier that religion begins when we realize our dependence upon God. When we are at the end of our resources, when we face disaster, disease, and death, there is nowhere to turn but to God. However, much of the time things go smoothly and we forget that "it is he that hath made us, and not we ourselves." Our usual mood was well expressed by the little boy who, when he came in his "Now I lay me" to the phrase "And help Jimmie be a good boy," remarked, "I guess I won't say that; I've done pretty well today by myself."

SECOND, WE SO OFTEN LEAVE GOD OUT OF LARGE AREAS OF

---

[6] *What Is Vital in Religion* (New York: Harper & Bros., 1955), page 66.

LIFE. The business or laboring man may be faithful in church attendance and private devotions; but if he never thinks of God in relation to the processes of making a living to which he devotes most of his waking hours, it is small wonder that God becomes unreal. The house-wife may teach a Sunday-school class and lead devotions at the woman's society, but if she does not seek God's will in the problems of her wifely and motherly tasks, he will become "an oblong blur." The active member of the youth fellowship will find that God becomes increasingly real only as he is taken into the relations of friendship, school, and vocational decision.

A THIRD SOURCE OF RELIGIOUS DULLNESS IS THE FAILURE TO ESTABLISH WHAT HAVE BEEN WELL CALLED "HOLY HABITS" OF DEVOTION. In the last generation or so there has been a healthy insistence that the Christian life did not consist in pious observances, but in a life of devoted service to God and man. In making this shift from the interior to the exterior aspects of religion, many left no place for practices of devotion. They failed to understand Jesus' remark, "These you ought to have done, without neglecting the others" (Matthew 23:23 R.S.V.). They did not distinguish the relationship between the roots and the fruits of religion. Our Protestant fathers had a sound insight when they called church attendance, the sacraments, private Bible reading, and prayer the "means of grace." These practices of personal devotion are not the *ends* of religious living; they are its *means*.

Eugene Carson Blake, then president of the National Council of Churches and stated clerk of the Presbyterian

35

Church, U.S.A., told an interdenominational National Convention of Christian men:

> The crucial question that every serious Christian must ask himself is, "How do I find out what Jesus Christ wants me to do?" I give you no new answers but repeat the ancient and tried conclusions of the Christian church: Every man must surrender himself to Jesus Christ as his own Lord and Savior. In short he must be converted. He must seek Christ's will through reading and study of the Bible. There is no other way. He must pray at the beginning and ending of each day, and in fellowship with his Christian brethren every week in the worship of the church. He must in the fellowship of the church receive the sacrament by which means Christ can be a very part of him. *These are the traditional "means of grace" and there is no short cut, no gadget, no automation technique by which they can be avoided.*[7]

IV

What then shall we do to be Christian in personal life? FIRST OF ALL, WE WILL TEST THE SINCERITY AND DEPTH OF OUR COMMITMENT TO CHRIST AS LORD. Is our life truly centered in God as he comes to us in Christ? Have we allowed this basic loyalty to God and Christ to affect every aspect and area of our living? Perhaps we experi-

---

[7] Quoted in *The Christian Century*, October 3, 1956, page 1127. Copyright by the Christian Century Foundation and reprinted by permission.

ence a feeling of warm devotion to Christ, but do we
have his mind and do we do the things he said? We may
know all the answers in the catechism and assent to all
the creeds, but do we love God with all our being and
our neighbors as ourselves? It may be that we are active
in many good causes for social betterment, but are
we kind and charitable to those who differ with us, do
we refuse to gossip, do we control our temper, and do
we truly trust God rather than our own efforts? Our
personal Christian living will become vital when we
realize that without God we "start at no beginning and
work toward no end."

SECOND, WE WILL KEEP ALIVE OUR SENSE OF NEED. This
does not mean that we shall live in a perpetual state
of crisis. Perhaps only in the midst of natural catastrophe
or historic conflict can the sense of imminent destruction
be maintained. But there is a normal and continuing fact
that without God we cannot sustain life for a single
moment. When our eyes open from sleep, we can
remind ourselves that the new day is his day and that
without his care in light, air, and food we could not live.
When we close our eyes at night, we can remember to
commit to him the cares and mistakes of the day. Perhaps
our deepest need, after all, is not for strength to face
the disasters of life, but for help to be the person God
meant us to be.

OUR PERSONAL RELIGION, IN THE THIRD PLACE, WILL TAKE
ON ADDED REALITY WHEN WE BECOME AWARE THAT GOD'S
WILL MUST RULE EVERY AREA OF OUR LIVES. It is significant
that Jesus used the example of home and family life to

give meaning to his teaching about the kingdom of God. Surely if we can be Christian anywhere, it will be in the home. Family relations between husband and wife, parents and children, brothers and sisters, offer the first school in which we can learn what it means to love one another even as Christ has loved us and where we can "bear one another's burdens" (R.S.V.). Outside the home constantly widening circles of friendship call for the practice of Christian understanding and good will. The realms of commerce and industry, science and art, too long have been regarded as a no man's land outside the rule of Christian love. Our religion will become both personal and vital as we seek to bring these aspects of experience under its sway. The latter portions of this study will consider what it means to be Christian in some of these specific areas of life.

FINALLY, OUR PERSONAL RELIGIOUS LIFE WILL TAKE ON ADDED DEPTH AS WE MAKE OUR OWN THOSE "HOLY HABITS" OF PRIVATE AND PUBLIC WORSHIP WHICH NURTURE AND FEED THE SPIRITUAL LIFE. As a young tree grows into the sky, it deepens and widens its root structure in the earth. In the same way if we desire to become mature Christians bearing the rich fruits of religious faith, we must put down our roots into that soil of devotion which has nourished the great souls that have gone before us.

FOR THOUGHT AND DISCUSSION

Read Romans 12. What help does this chapter give in knowing what it means to be Christian in personal life?

What specific directions do you find? Do these cover all conceivable decisions you might have to make? Do you find any general principles stated? What are they? How are they helpful?

Consider the relation between personal and social religion. Define each. Do you agree that the two emphases should not be separated? Do you know people who do separate them? What is the result? Are people more likely to stress personal religion and neglect the social or the reverse?

Three common conceptions of personal Christianity are described: the "carbon copy," the "rule book," and the "what would Jesus do?" schools of thought. Are any of these views prevalent in your community? Do you agree that these conceptions are inadequate? Why?

How does thinking of being a Christian as "a life of fellowship with God in Christ" differ from the three ideas above? What does this phrase mean to you?

Is it true that many people today do not so much think God untrue as find him unreal? How do you account for this? Make a list of the things that keep God from seeming real to our generation. How would living a life of fellowship with God in Christ overcome this?

What place does the observance of certain "holy habits" have in personal religion? What beyond this is required by being Christian in individual life?

What current situations can you think of where Christians differ as to what attitudes, beliefs, and actions should be expected of Christians? How can we be sure that we are being Christian in these areas?

CHAPTER 4

Being a Christian in Social Life

"IF RELIGION ENDS WITH THE INDIVIDUAL, IT ENDS." WE have seen that being a Christian involves an act of personal commitment to Christ as Lord. This in turn results in the reorganization of all aspects of the individual's life—feeling, thinking, acting—around Christ as the center. If it is true that "unless religion begins with the individual, it doesn't begin," why is not this the end of the matter?

I

IT MUST BE ADMITTED AT ONCE THAT MANY CHRISTIANS BELIEVE THAT PERSONAL RELIGION IS ALL THAT IS NEEDED. The aim of Christian evangelism, they believe, should be the conversion of individuals. These regenerated persons will, it is felt, automatically be changed in their social relationships. Thus the realm of politics, industry, and art will be brought under Christ's sway, and no special effort to make a social application of Christianity is necessary.

The magazine section of a Chicago Sunday newspaper carried a "letter to a church board" signed by Bruce Barton, prominent author and advertising executive. Mr. Barton had been aroused by a question on a recommendation form he had been asked to fill out for a young preacher. The question read: Is the preacher adroit at relating his preaching to the social and economic problems of the day?

Mr. Barton's response was that since he and millions of other Americans are confronted with social and economic problems all week, they go to church Sunday morning wanting to hear about something else, namely, about God. He went on to suggest that housing problems must have been pretty bad in Palestine, yet Jesus did not advocate slum clearance or federal housing projects. Likewise, there were labor problems, but Jesus did not become a labor organizer. Hunger and poverty were acute, yet Jesus did not organize bread lines or press for social security legislation. In short, since Jesus did not come to grips with social issues, his modern representative should preach God and not dabble in such mundane matters as housing, unemployment, hunger, or distribution of wealth.

At first glance this attitude will appeal to some persons. It is true that Jesus did not employ the techniques of a twentieth-century social reformer. Yet it is clear that Jesus was concerned about the social relations among the people of his day. He spoke out vigorously against the selfish accumulation of riches and the lack of concern for the poor on the part of some who were rich, he drove out the

41

money changers from the Temple, he denounced the wickedness of those in high places, he was concerned about the sanctity of marriage, and he condemned the collecting of excessive taxes.

Recall also that Jesus and the first generation of Christians lived and worked under a ruthless totalitarian dictatorship. Troops were quartered everywhere. The people had no voice whatever in the government. Their opinions were not asked; they were not wanted.

How different is the situation of twentieth-century Christians in the Western world! Nineteen centuries of Christian history have produced the democratic state where the citizens themselves are sovereign. Instead of being a slave or subject, the modern Western Christian is responsible through his vote and participation in political life for determining the policies of government. Thus in our times the individual Christian has not only the responsibility but the duty of social action.

II

NEVERTHELESS, THE VIEW PERSISTS THAT IT IS SOMEHOW IMPROPER FOR THE CHURCH TO SPEAK ON SOCIAL AND POLITICAL MATTERS OR FOR CHRISTIANS TO TAKE ORGANIZED GROUP ACTION IN THESE AREAS. The Church's proper sphere, it is held by some, is the conversion of individuals and the cultivation of the personal spiritual life. This view was cogently expressed by a group of churchmen in a statement:

We believe that regenerated men and women will, under proper guidance, endeavor to shape our social and economic fabric in each generation so as to implement the will of God on earth. . . . Through intimate personal relationship of the individual with God, there comes a richer experience in life, a recognition of God as Father, and of all men as brothers. Christ's spirit is that of love; men filled with His spirit are concerned for the welfare of their fellow men and seek to promote justice and mercy in the social, economic, and political order. The Methodist Church would enthrone Christ in the heart and life of the individual and thus infuse His spirit into the whole social order.[1]

There is an important truth in this statement. As we have seen, Christianity does begin with the individual's commitment to Christ as Lord, and this radical reorganization of life should affect every area of experience. *Unfortunately, however, this commitment does not automatically awaken the individual to every social implication of his actions.*

In contrast to the preceding quotation consider this statement from the Social Creed of The Methodist Church:

The interest of The Methodist Church in social welfare springs from the gospel, and from the labors of John Wesley, who ministered to the phys-

---

[1] From a statement by the Committee for the Preservation of Methodism quoted in *Is There a Pink Fringe in the Methodist Church?* page 1.

ical, intellectual, and social needs of the people to whom he preached the gospel of personal redemption.

In our historic position we have sought to follow Christ in bringing the whole of life, with its activities, possessions, and relationships, into conformity with the will of God. . . . Jesus taught us to love our neighbors and seek justice for them. To be silent in the face of need, injustice, and exploitation is to deny him.

Consider also this statement adopted by the National Lutheran Council:

It is the duty of the church to shed the light of God's Word upon the social ills and moral diseases of the nation and of the world. There is no area of life, individual or collective, which is exempt from the law of God and which is not in desperate need of His regenerating gospel.[2]

In a sermon preached to his New York congregation in 1892 on the text "Ye are the salt of the earth," Dr. Charles H. Parkhurst confronted them with the corrupt alliance between crime and politics in that city. He justified his course of action with these words:

We speak of these things because it is our business as the pastor of a Christian church to speak of them. . . . The salt is here for a purpose. If your

---

[2] *The Christian in His Social Living* (Columbus, Ohio: Board of Christian Social Action of the American Lutheran Church, 1955), page 45.

Christianity is not vigorous enough to help save this country and this city, it is not vigorous enough to do anything toward saving you. . . . This is not bringing politics into the pulpit. . . . The particular political stripe of a municipal administration is no matter of our interest, and none of our business; but to strike at iniquity is a part of the business of the church, indeed, it is *the* business of the church.[3]

Perhaps the dynamic interplay among individual Christian conscience, the action of Christian groups and churches, and the general public mind can be understood by looking at a historic example. A century ago this nation was rent with conflict over human slavery. Today no one would speak for this institution, but then sincere Christians believed that slavery was part of God's will and defended it from Scripture. Churches divided over the issue. It required thirty years of public agitation and political debate, four years of war, a constitutional amendment, and appropriate legal enactments to end what all now agree was a moral evil. On both sides of the conflict the churches were quite properly active in advocating what they conceived to be the right. Many of those who defended slavery were sincere Christians; their background and training caused them to interpret slavery in a certain way. But "new occasions teach new duties," and we see that social institutions are so complex and our human motives so mixed that sometimes only heartache and travail can awaken the individual

---

[3] *My Forty Years in New York* (New York: The Macmillan Co., 1923), pages 112, 114, 115-16.

conscience. And sometimes force must restrain those who ignorantly, or mistakenly, or deliberately, do wrong.

Of course the churches and concerned Christians do not necessarily have the technical knowledge to solve every social and economic problem. But they do have the duty to serve as the conscience of society wherever human welfare is concerned. Thus in the late nineteenth century Charles H. Parkhurst aroused the churches of New York City to the corruption of Tammany Hall and led them in a crusade for civic decency. When flashlight photography was developed, Jacob Riis through a series of illustrated newspaper stories showed the nation what it was like to live in slum tenements—many of them owned by Christian people and churches. Votes for women, the abolition of child labor, the eight-hour day in industry, the right of labor to organize—all these and many other generally accepted reforms have been achieved, not by the conversion of individuals alone, but by the devoted and often costly social action of concerned Christians and churches.

III

A religious life which was purely personal—confined to the practice of private devotions and evidenced only in immediate face to face relations—would be something less than Christian. WE ARE COMPELLED TO BRING ALL THE AREAS OF MAN'S SOCIAL LIFE UNDER THE SWAY OF CHRIST BY THE VERY NATURE OF THE CHRISTIAN FAITH. "Christ is Lord of all or he is not Lord at all!"

No man can live to himself alone. Because we are human, we are inevitably bound up with all the rest of mankind. A shot fired in some faraway place may involve all the world in war. Depressed farm prices bring unemployment to industrial workers. Substandard living conditions in a city slum bring disease, delinquency, and disorder to the entire community. This, of course, is not a uniquely Christian insight, but awareness of this truth is heightened when one sees all men as sinners for whom Christ died. Paul reminded the Athenian philosophers of our basic human unity when he said, "[God] made from one every nation of men to live on all the face of the earth" (Acts 17:26 R.S.V.).

Distinctly Christian is the conviction that *we must treat other men as God has treated us*. It is because God makes the sun to shine and the rain to fall on the unjust as well as the just (Matthew 5:45) that we must show evenhanded good will to all. If we love and do good only to those who love us, we do no better than pagans. We are to be perfect, as our heavenly Father is perfect (Matthew 5:46-48). The Christian answers the Old Testament question "Am I my brother's keeper?" by saying, "No, I am my brother's *brother.*"

Unique with Jesus was the understanding that *our moral obligation is not confined to the family who lives next door* or to the members of our own race, nation, or social group. The meaning of the story of the good Samaritan is that our neighbor is anyone in need. The last and the least of our fellow men is our neighbor. The golden rule might well be paraphrased to read:

47

I will desire and seek to secure for the children of the last and least family on earth what I desire and seek to secure for my own children.

Nor is the obligation to neighbor confined to his spiritual needs. It is significant that when Jesus preached in his home-town synagogue, he chose for his text words of the prophet Isaiah announcing good news to the poor, release to the captives, recovery of sight to the blind, and liberty to the oppressed (Luke 4:16-21; Isaiah 61:1). In his own ministry Jesus not only preached about God, but he healed the sick, fed the hungry, denounced self-righteous, pious leaders who would not lift a finger to ease man's burdens (Matthew 23:4), and drove the money-changers from the Temple (Matthew 21:12-13). The needs of the entire man are the proper concern of Christian love.

Jesus taught his followers to pray, "Thy kingdom come. Thy will be done in earth, as it is in heaven." If this petition is more than pious language, if it represents the longing of our hearts as well as the words of our lips, we are bound to spend ourselves unsparingly in the correction of every situation which is contrary to God's will for men and in the establishment of justice and righteousness in every area of life.

> Then let us prove our heavenly birth
> In all we do and know,
> And claim the kingdom of the earth
> For Thee, and not Thy foe.[4]

---

[4] By John Ellerton.

IV

IN OUR TIMES A DIMENSION HAS BEEN ADDED TO THE SOCIAL SIDE OF RELIGION BY THE COMPLEX AND IMPERSONAL NATURE OF MANY ASPECTS OF OUR COMMON LIFE. My grandfather was a partner and manager in a woolen mill which employed less than a hundred men. He knew them all by name and was intimately aware of their personal problems and family needs. He could be Christian in economic life on a personal, face to face basis. Contrast the situation of a person today who owns some shares of stock in a great industrial corporation. He is an owner and therefore responsible for the conditions which prevail within the industry. However, it is likely he has never seen the inside of even one of the company's many plants and knows nothing of the conditions or nature of employment that prevail there. Or think of the directors or management of the same corporation. Decisions which these men make may affect the lives and hopes of multitudes they do not know and never see. Because those powerful and impersonal organizations have such potential for the happiness or misery of mankind, the Christian must be concerned with the structure of society no less than with the character of the individual.

To correct abuses and injustices in these areas that are beyond personal knowledge and to bring them under responsible control, it is now widely recognized that the Christian conscience must support and demand such measures as commissions supervising the railroads, banks, communications, and the security exchange, and provision for unemployment compensation, old age security, and similar safeguards. To state some of the convictions of Christians in these matters, the churches have adopted a Social Creed. It has become clear that in such human concerns as represented by international relations, industrial policies, racial tensions, and political problems, the Christian really has only two options. Either he may regard these areas as outside God's concern, or he must accept responsibility for informed and concerted effort to bring them under Christian judgment and standards.

Perhaps the relation of personal and social responsibility can be seen by considering the automobile. Can you tell a Christian from a non-Christian by watching the drivers at a busy intersection? Does every regenerated person automatically become a careful, law-abiding operator of his car? *Is it likely that we would rely on the conversion of reckless drivers as the sole means of bringing the carnage on our highways under control?* Watching a young mother trying to get two children across the ceaseless traffic of a summer Sunday afternoon suggested a "parable of the Traffic Light."

A certain young mother on a hot Sunday afternoon decided to go down to the beach. With a baby buggy in one hand and her three-year-old in the other she came to the intersection of Sheridan Road. But lo, a vast stream of traffic was moving steadily in both directions. Among these travelers was an evangelist. Seeing the woman, he said to himself, Some day I must hold a meeting on this corner and convert some of these motorists so they will become considerate and let pedestrians pass. But now I must hurry, or I shall be late to my tent meeting in Zion City.

Another driver was chairman of the Official Board of the Born Again Methodist Church, but he could not hold up all this traffic for one woman and her children. People would think him queer! Thus an hour passed, and in all that throng not one took pity on the young mother's plight.

But there chanced to pass that way a traffic engineer. Rapidly he computed the number of potential pedestrians in the neighborhood, made a traffic count, and said: Let us erect here a traffic light so that at the flashing of the red, the yellow, and the green this woman and her friends may pass safely to the beach. And it was so even as he said.

FOR THOUGHT AND DISCUSSION

Read Luke 4:16-21. In what way does this passage point to social concern and action as the duty of the Christian? What other biblical passages and incidents can you think of which show that Christian faith is social as well as personal?

The slavery controversy is cited as an example of a social issue on which the Church has arrived at agreement as to a Christian position. Can you think of any others? On what social issues is there currently division in the churches?

Should the churches be silent on issues when they are in disagreement? Should they be silent when they do not have the technical information necessary for a solution?

Is it the function of the church to indicate solutions? What is the proper function of the church in social questions?

How does the example of the automobile illuminate the problems that are involved in bringing social conditions under the rule of the Christian conscience?

What is the Social Creed of the churches? (Methodists should consult Paragraph 2020 in the *Discipline*. Others should secure the Social Creed from the appropriate denominational agencies or the National Council of Churches.) What social questions are dealt with in this statement? What positions does it affirm as Christian? Are the members of your church aware of this creed? Do they agree with it? Are its positions accepted in the economic and social life of your community? What are some points of disagreement? What can you do to awaken the conscience of the community where it is not accepted?

CHAPTER 5

Being Christian in Family Life

IF A CHRISTIAN CAN BE DESCRIBED AS ONE WHO LOVES GOD with all his heart, mind, and strength and his neighbor as himself, the question might then be asked, "How does one learn to do this?" The answer is bound to be, "This is most likely to be learned at home." If an awareness of our dependence upon the overarching love and care of God is not absorbed unconsciously from our earliest experiences in the home, this conviction will be gained later only with great difficulty. If the sense of obligation for others is not learned in family relations with parents, brothers, and sisters, it will only rarely be learned at all.

So true is this that the great Egyptologist James Henry Breasted wrote in summarizing what he had learned from a lifetime of investigating the dawn of history:

> The surviving documents demonstrate histor-
> ically that the thing which was long called "the
> moral consciousness of mankind" has grown up

with each generation out of the discipline and the emotions of family life, supplemented by reflection and the teaching of experienced elders. The supreme values which lie within the human soul have therefore, as a matter of historical fact, entered the world for the first time through the operation of those gentle and ennobling influences which touch us continually in our family life. . . . It was the sunshine and the atmosphere of the earliest human homes that created ideals of conduct and revealed the beauty of self-forgetfulness.[1]

What was true in the earliest civilization is still true. Thus Hartshorne and May in their classic study of the sources of character ascribed 8 per cent to the influence of the church, 8 per cent to the public schools, mostly exerted by a few strong teachers, but the home was found to be determinative. It is not strange then that Jesus chose the relationship between father and children to illuminate his thought about our relation to God and that he used the figure of brotherly love within the family to show us how we ought to live with one another. *If we do not manage to be Christian at home, we are not likely to manage it anywhere.*

I

There are many reasons why it is important that we give earnest consideration to being Christian in home and family life. FOR ONE THING, WE HAVE JUST NOTED

---

[1] *The Dawn of Conscience* (New York: Chas. Scribner's Sons, 1933), pages 410-11. Used by permission of the publisher.

THAT JESUS USED FAMILY LIFE TO ILLUSTRATE HIS UNDER-
STANDING OF THE CHARACTER OF GOD. Suppose, for example,
that a child hears the story of the prodigal son in church
school or that a man who has lost his way hears this
story told in a sermon. Suppose also, that these persons
have never experienced love and understanding in their
relations with their human fathers, but rather have re-
ceived unreasonable demands, or indifference, or even
cruelty. Under such circumstances how can the loving
forgiveness of a father God be convincing? Or how can
a quarrelsome, loveless home, where each child is a
ruthless rival of his brothers and sisters for the satisfaction of his needs, be a symbol of the loving concern for
others which Christianity holds up as the ideal of social
life? The home and family life we knew as children and
which we supply for our own children make Christian
faith easy or difficult.

AGAIN, THE BASIC SET OF A PERSON'S CHARACTER IS CHIEFLY
GIVEN BY HIS HOME. The friendship group in which we
move is important, but we are likely to select those
friends from people congenial to our home standards.
The public schools are rightly concerned about character
education, but they must work with boys and girls whose
ideas of right and wrong have already been largely
formed in the home. The church tries to motivate unselfish, other-regarding conduct, but this is difficult—we
might say well-nigh impossible—unless the appeal can
build upon attitudes learned at home. In fact, wherever
society breaks down—as in juvenile delinquency, crime,
a betrayal of trust by public officials, racketeering, or

indifference to the rights of others—there is likely to be found a character failure traceable to the home.

FURTHERMORE, THE CENTRAL VALUES WHICH OUR SOCIETY CHERISHES ARE LEARNED AT HOME. We like to think of ourselves as a democratic nation, but where does democracy begin? If the homes of the nation are authoritarian, if differences of opinion within families are not respected, if the strong in the family do not regard the needs of the weak, how can we expect the democratic ideal to be realized in the community and nation? The democratic state is simply one which seeks to realize the ideal of Christian family relations in the total life of the community.

Concern is often expressed at the materialistic character of contemporary life. Some years ago a Gallup poll reported that the eight things most desired by Americans were in this order: automobile, house, clothes, household equipment, permanent peace, personal health, money, and job security. Do these represent the real desires of the American people? Only one of these, permanent peace, might be called a spiritual value, but a moment's reflection will show that without peace none of the other desires is ultimately possible. And what about our need to love and be loved, the ancient passion for liberty of thought, action, and worship? What of the necessity to find work in which we can express our individuality and find self-respect and the respect of our comrades? *If Americans no longer want these spiritual values but have become obsessed with the desire for material things, have they learned this in their homes?* If it is important that they hold more spiritual ideas of what life can offer, will they gain them anywhere if not in the experiences of family life?

A nationally famous tax lawyer was offered a large fee if he would write an opinion favoring the interests of a certain group. He refused to do so. When asked why, he replied that his decision traced back to an incident of his boyhood and the way his mother handled a situation involving a nickel he had found! So far-reaching are the simple incidents of home and family life!

II

The establishment of Christian homes may be important, but it is not easy. *Our culture puts the major responsibility for the quality of home life upon the wife and mother.* We call her the "homemaker." Modern economic life takes most men out of the home, and often out of the community, for long hours each day. This puts an inordinate demand upon the woman to set the standards of the home, make plans for family life, exercise discipline, and manage and maintain the residence in addition to the older skills of providing for the food and clothing of the household. It is to the everlasting credit of American women that most of them do so well in carrying more than their share of family responsibility.

However, it is one of the tragedies of modern life that just when the demands of homemaking are the greatest, women are least willing to regard this as an important and satisfying vocation. Exciting careers are now open to them in business and the professions. It is common to hear a woman participant on a radio or television show say, "Oh, I'm just a housewife," as if this were an occupation without prestige or importance. Furthermore, in many homes the desires and wants which must be satisfied "to keep up with" the community require a second income, and the wife goes to work. Often this is done at the beginning of marriage so that both husband and wife can have the satisfaction of contributing to the purchase of house, furniture, and car. However, as they become accustomed to a double income, it is harder and harder to scale down their wants to one salary.

FOR WOMEN BEING CHRISTIAN AT HOME WOULD SEEM TO REQUIRE A RETHINKING OF WHAT A FAMILY REALLY NEEDS TO BE HAPPY, A DISCOVERY OF THE IMPORTANCE OF HOMEMAKING AS A CHRISTIAN VOCATION, AND A GLAD ACCEPTANCE OF THEIR ROLE AS WIFE AND MOTHER. On the fiftieth anniversary of her graduation Smith College conferred an honorary doctor's degree upon Mrs. Harry Emerson Fosdick. The citation read:

> Her career is one that is basic to our society. As wife and as mother she has been many things— teacher, nurse, business woman, philosopher and spiritual comforter. Her talents have been used to help build the lives of her husband and her children, and through them, as well as through her own participation, she has served her church, her community, her country, her world.[2]

---

[2] Harry Emerson Fosdick, *The Living of These Days* (New York: Harper & Bros., 1956), page 81. Used by permission of the publisher.

THE MAJOR DIFFICULTY FOR THE MAN IN MAKING HIS CONTRIBUTION TO CHRISTIAN HOME LIFE LIES IN THE DISPLACEMENT OF THE HOME AT THE CENTER OF HIS LIFE BY THE DEMANDS OF HIS FUNCTION AS BREADWINNER. He is not so much husband and father as he is pay check and meal ticket. The religion of Abraham, Isaac, and Jacob derived from a rural economy where these patriarchs exercised their economic and their familial responsibilities at the same time and the same place. They were truly priests to their families. Boys raised on the farm today still have the advantage of working side by side with their fathers and learning their standards and values from them.

However, in most American homes the children see their father in the morning, if at all, in a mad dash for work, and in the evening he is often too physically and nervously exhausted to enter creatively into the life of the home and the interests of wife and children. All too frequently the more successful a man becomes as businessman, the less successful he is as husband and father. Many a man has awakened too late to the realization that no success in the economic world can compensate for a failure in the family world.

One young Christian layman was forging rapidly ahead in the sales organization of a great corporation, but he suddenly discovered that the price of this success was less and less time for wife and children. After a long struggle with himself he declined a promotion and left the company's employ in order to take a much less demanding—and less remunerative—job with a small firm. He did this, he said, so that he might have time for his family, his church, and for some civic responsibility. Doubtless not all Christian men will have to make such rigorous decisions—any more than all Jewish men were asked to sell all they possessed to follow Jesus. However, there is need for much clear and honest thinking as to the role of the Christian man in family life.

CHILDREN ALSO HAVE THEIR PART IN THE CREATION OF CHRISTIAN HOMES. The fifth commandment directs us to honor our fathers and mothers, but what this means is not spelled out. Certainly more is involved than the passive obedience of parental commands. Children, no less than adults, can be either selfish or unselfish, considerate of others or insistent upon their own desires. Bickering, quarrelsome, un-co-operative children can make a home a hell, even as thoughtful, happy, generous children can make it seem like heaven. The admonition that we must become as little children in order to enter the kingdom of heaven must mean at least that in their simple, uncalculating attitudes children have a basic contribution to make to our common life.

In the Christian home husband, wife, and children are engaged in a mutual give and take in which the interests and needs of each are reconciled and united by their common acceptance of the lordship of Christ. Consider, for example, the Christian ideal of family life presented in Ephesians 5:1-6:4. The Christian family is one which walks in love, where each gives himself for the others as Christ loved and gave himself for the Church.

The Christian avoids lust and indulgence, lives in purity before marriage and in faithfulness afterward. Wives are to be subject to their husbands, but these are husbands who nourish and cherish their wives as they do their own bodies. Children are to obey their parents, but these are parents who will not provoke their children to anger. Such homes will be what Henry S. Canby called "the most impressive experience in life."

III

What makes a home a Christian home? What is expected of the members of the family group if they are to be Christian in family life? FIRST OF ALL, OF COURSE, EACH MEMBER OF THE FAMILY WILL BE A CHRISTIAN IN HIS PERSONAL COMMITMENT. It takes Christians to make a Christian home. It is loyalty to God as he comes to us in Christ that removes self from the center of life and enables selfish people to become unselfish, thoughtless people to become kind and considerate. We are told that "the fruit of the Spirit is love, joy, peace, patience, kindness, goodness, faithfulness, gentleness, self-control" (Galatians 5:22 R.S.V.). These are obviously the characteristics which will mark a Christian family. Love is the basic Christian attribute, and we are told that

> . . . love is patient and kind; love is not jealous or boastful; it is not arrogant or rude. Love does not insist on its own way; it is not irritable or resentful; it does not rejoice at wrong, but rejoices in the right. Love bears all things, believes all things,

hopes all things, endures all things. (I Corinthians 13:4-7 R.S.V.)

Can you think of a finer description of the spirit which should pervade a Christian home? Common devotion to such ideals makes a home Christian.

SECOND, A CHRISTIAN HOME IS ONE WHERE THE RIGHTS OF ALL—LITTLE AND BIG, WEAK AND STRONG—ARE RESPECTED. This has suggested to many the family conference as a method of deciding problems which affect the whole family. Some families schedule a regular weekly time for these conferences—perhaps after dinner Monday night—and each member of the family group is expected to bring up any matters he wants discussed. Others call a conference only when something needs decision. Everything from who should help with the dishes to the family budget is open for consideration and decision by the family conference. Often when crucial matters have been decided, perhaps involving the giving up of a treasured desire by some member of the family, wise parents may lift the experience to the level of worship and prayer. A great American writes in his biography:

Many a time in later years, hearing expounded some new, progressive idea concerning the rearing of children, I have wondered why it was called new, because it was the familiar method of my childhood's home. We were a democratic family from the start. Among my earliest recollections are family conferences where all of us were called together to talk over some problem which concerned the whole household. We youngsters were invited to say what we thought. . . .

Religion was a force in our family rather than a form, but it was always there, vital and real, and I recall yet some special occasions when family prayers made movingly explicit the unity and loyalty of the home.[3]

THIRD, A CHRISTIAN HOME IS ONE WHERE THE BIBLE IS READ AND LOVED. It is as difficult to think of Christian character growing apart from the soil of the Bible as it is to conceive of fruit without the orchard. There are many ways in which the Bible may become part of family life. Well-chosen Bible stories will be read to children, perhaps from such a source as Walter Russell Bowie's *Story of the Bible*. Young people will be introduced to one or more of the exciting translations into modern speech such as those by Moffatt, Goodspeed, or J. B. Phillips. Both individual and group reading will be encouraged. An attractive, well-bound copy of the new Revised Standard Version may form the basis of family worship experiences.

FOURTH, CERTAIN "HOLY HABITS" WILL BE ENCOURAGED AS AN ASPECT OF CHRISTIAN HOME LIFE. The offering of thanks at mealtime is certainly a minimum observance. To recognize daily that God is indeed the source of "every good gift and every perfect gift" is to nourish that sense of dependence which we have seen is basic to religious living. Family devotions at the morning or

[3] Fosdick, *op. cit.*, pages 32, 36.

evening meal is a time-tested practice for deepening the spiritual life of the home. If guidance is needed, there are many helps such as a section each month in *The Christian Home,* the *Book of Worship for Church and Home,* or devotional booklets provided by most of the denominations, such as *The Upper Room* by the Methodists and *Today* by the Presbyterians.

FIFTH, SOME FAMILIES HAVE FOUND IT HELPFUL TO MAKE THE CHRISTIAN ORIENTATION OF THE HOME EXPLICIT BY ERECTING A WORSHIP CENTER in some central place in the house. This may take the form of a good religious picture above a small table on which are an open Bible, candles, and flowers. Whatever its detail, it will serve to remind visitors, as well as members of the family, that here is a home where Christ is loved and God is served in obeying the commandment "that ye love one another."

SIXTH, A CHRISTIAN FAMILY WILL BE A CHURCH-GOING FAMILY. Just as individuals need the support of the family if they are to be Christian, so families need the support of the larger Christian community. The development of age-group programs in the church school for each stage of the child's growth has made a great contribution to better religious instruction for children and youth. However, if attendance at these sessions replaces family participation in the corporate worship of the church, particularly if children are sent to church school while parents go to neither school nor church, an important unifying experience has been lost from the home. A later chapter will discuss being Christian in church relations. It is enough to point out here that religious instruction is not a substitute for worship and that the common worship of the entire church is the one point where the Christian community bridges all differences of age, class, and moral condition to acknowledge mutual dependence upon God.

In the early nineteenth century when many Germans looked to America as the promised land, Goethe said to his countrymen, "Here [that is, in Germany] or nowhere is America." Tolstoy expressed the same idea in a tale about a Russian peasant who went on a long and fruitless pilgrimage to the Holy Land: "Your Jerusalem can be in your own village." Similarly many who long for a Christian world will find that Christian society is waiting to be created in their own homes. *The kingdom of God begins at home!*

FOR THOUGHT AND DISCUSSION

Scripture background: Read Ephesians 5:1-6; also Colossians 3:18-21. Do these passages throw light on the attitudes and relationships that make a home Christian? In what ways do they correspond with or differ from prevailing customs in American home life?

What are the points of greatest disagreement or conflict in American family life—between husbands and wives, between parents and children, between brothers and sisters? Does the Christian ideal of personal and social life help solve these problems? Do the biblical passages cited above point to the easing or the intensifying of points of difficulty in contemporary homes?

What is the New Testament ideal of home and family life? The following passages may help:

Jesus' statement of the marriage ideal: Mark 10:2-9.

The apostles married: I Corinthians 9:5.

Purity before marriage and faithfulness after marriage: I Thessalonians 4:3-7 and many other passages.

Interpersonal relations in the home: Colossians 3:18-21; Ephesians 5:21–6:4.

A committee might draft a statement for class discussion and revision of the Christian view of marriage and family life. In preparing this consult official church pronouncements such as *The Methodist Discipline,* Paragraph 2021. If a good statement results from your class discussion, release it to the local press, or a panel discussion of the Christian home might be arranged over a local radio station.

What resources are available in the community for preparing young people for marriage? For counseling families who are in difficulty? Does your local church do anything in this area?

What is the accepted division of home duties in your community as between husbands and wives, parents and children? How might these customary practices be criticized from a Christian standpoint?

Have any members of the group had experience with the family conference? How is this conducted? What kinds of problems are dealt with? Is it helpful? How does the family conference help children make a larger contribution to building a Christian home? Could you prepare a dramatization of a family conference for presentation at some church occasion?

Invite a sharing of experiences as to the observance of "holy habits" of the Christian family life. What practices are helpful? How can their wider observance be promoted in your church?

Is *Christian Home* circulated among the young parents in your church? Secure some sample copies from The Methodist Publishing House, Nashville, Tennessee, discuss the contents of this excellent periodical, and consider how more use of it might be made in your parish.

Many churches seek to deepen the unity of family life and relate families more intimately with the church by holding occasional family nights with a common meal, family worship, study groups, and a program of interest to all. Could your church do anything of this kind?

CHAPTER 6

Being Christian in Friendship

IN CONVERSATION WITH HER PASTOR A YOUNG MATRON IN an upper middle-class suburb said: "You know, we have so much entertaining we have to do in connection with my husband's business that I never really feel free to make new friends. Most of these people I don't feel close to, and yet it is essential to my husband's career that we mix with them socially."

· · · · ·

A young person who made a brilliant beginning in the entertainment world was quoted as saying: "I have hundreds of acquaintances but no friends. If I should 'fall on my face,' they would all disappear."

· · · · ·

Tom and Mary are a brother and sister of high-school age whose family moved to a new community. Tom, who was an outstanding athlete at his former school, had no difficulty in making friends in his new home, but Mary, somewhat shy and retiring, found that all the girls her age already had their friendship groups and showed no interest in her.

. . . . .

Mr. and Mrs. Tomarek, a refugee family from Central Europe, met the pastor of big First Church at a P.T.A. meeting and in response to his invitation came with their three children to church the following Sunday. Except for the pastor no one paid any attention to them, and the children were ignored in the classes to which they were assigned. After two or three Sundays the Tomareks gave up the effort to become a part of First Church.

. . . . .

These and many other examples you could add from your own observation serve to underline the world's need for friendship. But each one of us needs friendship also. *If we are to become complete human beings, we must find acceptance, respect, and affection from others whose approval is important to us.* This sense of belonging we get from our friends.

In one of his books Dr. Harry Emerson Fosdick speaks of "the lonely individual, poor in personal relationships, who feels all shut up within himself," and he quotes Thackeray as saying, "How lonely we are in the world! how selfish and secret, everybody! . . . Ah, sir—a distinct universe walks about under your hat and under mine—

. . . you and I are but a pair of infinite isolations, with some fellow-islands a little more or less near to us." [1] All such persons stand in need of friendship if they are to be rescued—as do you and I if we are to escape—from such isolation.

I

The experience of friendship offers us a natural arena for practicing Christian relations with others. Being Christian in the home has its problems, to be sure; but parents, brothers, and sisters are at least the persons nearest and dearest to us with whom it should be easiest to establish relations of Christian love and good will. The circle of personal relationships outside the home is the one where friendships are formed and where our ability to meet others in the spirit of Christ will meet its first test. Are there any Christian principles to guide us as we try to be friends and make friends?

1. CHRISTIANS SHOULD BEGIN BY REMEMBERING THAT WE ARE TO TREAT OTHERS AS GOD HAS TREATED US. It is because God has not dealt with us according to our merits that we show good will to others. He makes the sun to shine on both the evil and the good, and when the rain cloud passes over, it asks no questions about the character of the person whose property lies below. For most of us this is a fortunate thing, and the wiser we grow the more we realize that what we want from God is not justice but mercy.

---

[1] *On Being a Real Person* (New York: Harper & Bros., 1943), pages 246, 248.

2. FURTHERMORE, CHRISTIANS KNOW THAT IN FRIENDSHIP AS IN ALL ELSE CHRIST IS OUR EXAMPLE. He was friend to the lowly and outcast as well as guest of the wealthy and prominent. He gave himself without reserve to all who were in need and yet had a special place of intimacy for the Twelve. Even at the hour of betrayal he addressed Judas as "Friend" (Matthew 26:50).

3. THE NATURE OF GOD AND THE EXAMPLE OF CHRIST COMBINE TO CONVINCE THE CHRISTIAN THAT LOVE IS THE LAW OF FRIENDSHIP AS OF LIFE. But this is not selfish love that seeks what it can get for itself. The death of friendship is the calculating attitude which says, "I'll scratch your back because I know you are going to scratch mine." Christian friendship is built on other-regarding love which "seeketh not her own."

4. CHRISTIANS BELIEVE THAT THE MOST IMPORTANT THING IN THE WORLD IS PERSONS. God did not create the world so that he could admire the scenery or collect chemical elements. He did so because he wanted fellowship with other spirits made in his image. Jesus asserted that the most sacred institution of his nation, the Sabbath, was made for man; man did not exist for the institution. Friends are important because people are important, more important than any wealth or success we can achieve.

5. CHRISTIAN FRIENDSHIP WILL BREAK THROUGH THE BARRIERS THAT USUALLY KEEP PEOPLE APART. Neither the worth nor the need of an individual is determined by his social class. In an age when outside marriage men and women had few social contacts, Jesus was a friend of women.

He accepted criticism for dining with "publicans and sinners," for, he said, the physician should go to the sick, not to the well. Jews had no dealings with Samaritans and as few as possible with Gentiles, yet Jesus numbered both among his friends. Christian friendship today should similarly break down walls that separate.

These, then, are the principles which ought to guide us as we seek to be Christian in our friendships.

II

Do these principles throw any light upon our problems in friendship? In fact, what are the difficulties we face most commonly in being Christian in friendship?

1. UNDOUBTEDLY OUR CENTRAL PROBLEM IS IN BEING THE KIND OF PERSON WHO CAN BE A FRIEND. The surest way to have friends is to be a friend. But to be a friend is exactly what some folks cannot do. They cannot be friends because they are too much wrapped up in themselves. And this is where a Christian principle comes in.

We saw above that love is the law of friendship. But there are two kinds of love. There is first of all the self-centered love which is interested in others only for what it can get out of them. A leading student of psychology from a Christian point of view writes:

> Selfishness is an attitude in which an individual's capacity for love is centered in himself in a childish manner. He then interprets the whole world and all of his experience in terms of whether or not it satisfies his particular needs and desires. . . . There

are many adults in whom this childish tendency to center all their affection in themselves is never outgrown. Their relationship to other people is constantly on the basis of what others do for them and never on the basis of what they may do for other people. It is all receive and no give.[2]

This kind of love kills friendship. However, there is another kind of love—other-regarding love, which is the natural product of the Christian's experience of God in Christ. This love takes its cue from the love of God, which goes out without limit to "all sorts and conditions of men." It is released by the love of Christ, who gave himself without reserve for all the children of men. *The person who has truly experienced God's love for him and who feels deeply that God will provide for all his needs is freed from self-love and enabled to show love to others.*

How do we learn to do this? C. S. Lewis, the popular British broadcaster on religious themes, writes:

The rule for all of us is perfectly simple. Don't waste time bothering whether you "love" your neighbour; act *as if you did.* As soon as we do this we find one of the great secrets. When you are behaving *as if* you loved someone, you will presently come to love him. . . . There is, indeed, one exception. If you do him a good turn, not to please God and obey the law of charity, but to show him what a fine forgiving chap you are, and to put him in

_____
[2] Carroll A. Wise, *Pastoral Counseling: Its Theory and Practice* (New York: Harper & Bros., 1951), page 153.

73

your debt, and then sit down to wait for his "gratitude," you will probably be disappointed. . . . But whenever we do good to another self, just because it is a self, made (like us) by God, and desiring its own happiness as we desire ours, we shall have learned to love it a little more or, at least, to dislike it less.[3]

2. A SECOND PROBLEM IS FINDING TIME FOR FRIENDSHIP. The Greens were delighted when they learned that Helen and Jack Carpenter had moved to town. Years ago, before either were married, the two couples had known each other at the state university. "We must have them over for dinner right away," said Edna Green to her husband when he told her the news. However, the next week was all filled, the following week George Green was to be away on a business trip, and after that there was a school play, a P.T.A. board meeting, an important business conference, and so on. On the few occasions when either of the Greens saw their old friends, they spoke vaguely of getting together soon, but somehow there was never a free date, and gradually what had once been a warm friendship became only a nodding acquaintance.

Most of us could add many stories from our own experience of friendships that withered or never had a chance to grow because we were too busy. Friendship is a flower that needs the soil of shared experience and the warmth of leisurely companionship. Multitudes are

---

[3] *Christian Behaviour* (New York: The Macmillan Co., 1943), pages 51-52. Used by permission of the publisher.

friendless today because they are too crowded by the demands of business, of the organizations to which they belong, and by the struggle to keep up appearances to have time for friends.

The principle involved here is that persons are important. We agree to this with our lips, but we deny it with our lives. Judged by our actions, we think that our careers are important, or our social position, our income, our advancement to the next highest office in the lodge, but not people. We see an acquaintance on the street, and even as we grasp his hand, we look over his shoulder at the corner clock to see if we are late for our next appointment. We have no time for friends. We put things above persons.

3. STILL ANOTHER PROBLEM AREA IN BEING CHRISTIAN IN FRIENDSHIP LIES IN THE NARROW RANGE FROM WHICH WE DRAW OUR FRIENDS. Perhaps nowhere do we fall further from the Christian ideal and the practice of Jesus. God sends his good gifts to all without regard to class, color, or creed. Jesus was despised because he consorted with the outcast. But we are careful to win approval by confining our friendships to those of our own kind, color, and social class. Our communities are full of interesting people who would enrich our lives, but we pass them by because they are "queer." Or again there are many who desperately need friends to give them assurance and hope. We might be those friends, but if we were, our crowd would think *us* queer.

A social fraternity at a Midwestern university pledged a young man whose father was a distinguished person and formerly an important official of a friendly foreign government. However, he was an Oriental. As the time for initiation approached, six other pledges informed the officers of the fraternity that if this Oriental joined, they would not. After several sessions the officers asked the young foreign student to depledge, which he did. Said the president of the group when interviewed by the press, "If you can't get members, you can't pay your bills, so what are you going to do?" Within days this story went around the world and appeared among other places with pictures on the front page of the Tokyo *Times. The failure of this group to enlarge the boundaries of its friendship to include a youth of different cultural background not only impoverished the lives of these young men and injured the spirit of the rejected person, but damaged the prestige of American civilization and played into the hands of Communist propaganda.*

Does this mean that it is wrong for Christians to have special friends chosen from people who have the same background and interests as themselves? By no means. Jesus gave his friendship to many people, but he chose twelve to be with him in a special way, and among these there were three who formed an inner circle. What is wrong is to become so engrossed in a little group of kindred spirits that we shut out many who need us and whom we need.

4. This matter of breaking barriers and enlarging our friendships to include persons outside the range of our normal contacts brings up another problem area, conflicting standards in friendship. Isn't it dan-

gerous to make friendships with people of different backgrounds and ideals? Granted that Jesus consorted with "publicans and sinners," isn't it risky for us, particularly for impressionable young people, to be too intimate with persons whose standards are different, perhaps lower, than ours?

Margaret had been told by her mother that she could not go with Hazel. But Margaret continued to eat lunch with her at school, they walked home together each afternoon to within a block of Margaret's home, and often managed to spend their evenings together when Margaret would get permission to go somewhere else. Talking about it to another girl one day, Margaret said, "I know that Hazel is loud, and mother says that she is boy crazy. Her parents aren't as nice as they should be either. But I don't think she has ever had a chance. She is anxious to do better as fast as she can learn, and she sticks to you through thick and thin. I think I ought to help her. If some of us don't watch out for her, no telling what will become of her."

Of course Margaret is not justified in deceiving her mother, but is she right in seeing the good in Hazel and trying to bring it out? Should Hazel be expected to reform first and then receive the friendship of persons of higher standards? Is Margaret wise in trying to reform Hazel as an individual project? Would she be better advised to bring Hazel into a group relationship where high standards of dress, manners, and behavior would have the support of group approval?

This story of Margaret and Hazel and the questions

it has raised force us to consider the nature of the church. *Is the church a shelter for saints or a school for sinners? Should the people who are fighting a losing battle with life be required to win their struggles outside the church, while all the nice people within the church ignore them?* There was a time when the church was a fellowship of friends, where the strong bore the burdens of the weak, the rich shared their substance with the poor, and all rejoiced with those who rejoiced and wept with those who wept. Can the church ever win the world unless it recovers this spirit of friendship for the lost and the least? Can your church be accurately described as a fellowship of friends?

III

We have seen that Christian friendship should break down the barriers that usually keep people apart, and we have considered the meaning of friendship for some of these areas of separation. There remains one barrier which is so significant in our culture that it deserves discussion by itself. This is the barrier of sex difference, which affects friendship between men and women. *We cannot deal honestly with the problems of being Christian unless we ask, What does it mean to be a Christian in the relationships of men and women?*

Although Jesus never married, the New Testament makes it clear that he had many friendly and constructive contacts with women. A group of women whom he had helped are named as contributing to the financial support of his ministry (Luke 8:1-3). The home of Mary and Martha in Bethany was one of his favorite stopping places. At least two incidents are related in detail where Jesus dealt redemptively with women of no reputation (John 4:7-30; 8:3-11). At the last it was a group of loving women who waited faithfully at the foot of the cross and prepared his body for burial, and it was to a woman that he first appeared on Easter Day.

This example of Jesus and his teaching as to the sacredness of human personality has provided the base from which the church has constructed its standard of Christian relations between the sexes. Persons are supremely important and are always to be treated with respect. A Christian will never use another person for his own selfish purposes. This means for both the Christian man and the Christian woman in their friendships with each other the practice of respect and consideration and a refusal of one to exploit the other.[4]

FROM THE EARLIEST TIMES THE TEACHING OF THE CHURCH HAS BEEN CLEAR THAT SEXUAL INTERCOURSE SHOULD BE CONFINED TO THE MARRIAGE RELATION. "Purity before marriage and faithfulness after marriage," is the way one well-known church leader, Alan Walker of Australia, puts it. Unfortunately a false Victorian modesty has until recent years prevented the church from helping its young people with clear and unequivocal teaching at this point. Consequently many of them have been thrown into

---

[4] Space does not permit going into questions of dating practices, courtship, and the selection of a life mate. Fortunately many excellent books in this area have been written. Your pastor or denominational youth department will be glad to suggest titles.

temptations of military service and enforced separation from home and friends without a clear understanding of the Christian ideal.

An army chaplain, home from two years of service in the Far East, writes angrily of the readiness of our servicemen to "shack up" with native women. "More than nine out of ten of the American servicemen marrying Japanese girls live with them as man and wife during the period of so-called courtship." One such youth, applying for permission to marry, admitted having sexual relations from his first date. Asked about his church background at home, he said, "I'm a Methodist. . . . I went to Sunday school some. But my folks were not too regular at church so I dropped out after a while." The chaplain continues:

> Yet he was a Methodist youth, a refugee from a Methodist Sunday school, who had no moral sense at all. He saw nothing wrong with what he'd done. Under pressure from me he came up with the same lame excuse they all used: "But everybody is doing the same thing." . . .
>
> Much has been said, pro and con, about the moral atmosphere of military service. And many people have been quick to point the accusing finger at the army, the navy and the air force. But it is my belief that the churches of America and the people who comprise their membership have not faced up to their responsibility.[5]

[5] Chaplain (Major) George H. Birney, "G.I. Morals—Whose Fault?" *The Christian Century*, January 11, 1956, page 44. Copyright by the Christian Century Foundation and reprinted by permission.

In the same vein Dr. Carl F. Yeager, associate secretary of the Lutheran Service Commission, told the National Lutheran Council recently that "young GIs are immoral overseas because cherished American institutions have failed them."

By 1960, Dr. Yeager estimated, 85 per cent of the nation's male churchgoers will have had some form of military training. This marks life in the armed forces as one of the most critical areas of Christian service in this generation. We cannot expect our youth to stand up to moral, political, and social pressures if the institutions in which they are nurtured failed them in their formative years.

The columns of almost any newspaper will reveal that finding a constructive basis for relationships between the sexes is as great a problem for civilian life as for the military. *The church can make a significant contribution to its solution by straightforward teaching of its youth and by providing programs where wholesome friendships between men and women are possible.*

Second only to the home, the experiences of friendship offer the training ground where the individual Christian can learn what it means to love his neighbor as himself and to practice such biblical admonitions as:

> Love one another with brotherly affection; outdo one another in showing honor. (Romans 12:10 R.S.V.)
>
> Therefore be imitators of God, as beloved chil-

dren. And walk in love, as Christ loved us and gave himself up for us. (Ephesians 5:1-2 R.S.V.)

This is my commandment, that you love one another as I have loved you. Greater love has no man than this, that a man lay down his life for his friends. (John 15:12 R.S.V.)

FOR THOUGHT AND DISCUSSION

Biblical background: Read I Samuel 18. David and Jonathan are a classic example of friendship. What things did Jonathan consider when he saw David? What material advantages did Jonathan's friendship secure for David? Do you suppose David thought of all this before he made a covenant with Jonathan?

Read Mark 3:13-19. Were these men Jesus chose to be with him accidental acquaintances, or were they selected after careful consideration? Why did Jesus choose these men for special intimacy and not others? Can you think of any later incidents where their actions must have been a trial to the Master? How did Jesus treat them in these situations? Was Jesus more concerned with what they were or what they might become? What do Jesus' relations with the disciples suggest for Christian friendship?

Jesus, friend of sinners: Matthew 9:10-13; 11:16-19; Luke 7:36-50.

Jesus' invitation to friendship: John 15:7-17.

The phrase, a fellowship of friends, is sometimes used as a description of the church. What does it suggest? In what ways does your church merit this description? In what ways does it fail to deserve it? What can you do to surround with Christian friendship those who are outside the fellowship of any church?

Do the principles enumerated in Section I suggest helpful criteria for evaluating friendship experiences? Apply them to some problems in friendship not discussed in the text. Can you think of other Christian principles that should be added to the list?

What problems in friendship do you and your friends have?

What is meant by the saying "Persons are always to be regarded as ends, not as means"? What does this say to friendship in general? What does it say about relations between men and women? In what ways do boys and girls, men and women, exploit one another (regard each other as means) in our society? How would our behavior be changed if we regarded one another as ends?

What adventures in friendship might you undertake?

CHAPTER 7

Being Christian at Work

IN THE EARLY DAYS OF WORLD WAR II AN ALMOST UNBELIEV-able event occurred. The responsible leaders of the Church of England, the Roman Church in England, and the Free Churches issued a joint statement concerning the religious foundations which must undergird an enduring peace. The ninth principle in this statement affirmed: "The sense of a divine vocation must be restored to man's daily work." More than a decade later the Second Assembly of the World Council of Churches underlined this judgment by setting up as one of its six major sections a commission on "The Laity: The Christian in His Vocation." The assembly said:

Today many people are asking whether Christianity has any relevance to their daily work. They feel that there is a gulf between the Church and its worship and their workaday lives. . . . It would appear that in comparison with the Church's effort to teach the application of the gospel to the life of the family and to personal relations, the effort to apply the gospel to the world of work has been relatively slight.[1]

I

Why do these Christian leaders think it so important that the world of daily work be seen in relation to the purposes of God? Some people might insist—indeed it has been often argued—that the realm of business, commerce, and industry is under the operation of automatic economic laws which remove it from moral and spiritual concern. Prices, it is urged, go up and down according to supply and demand. Wage rates and volume of employment rise and fall in reaction to market conditions. Crop surpluses on the farm and unemployment in the city involve no questions of right and wrong, but only of failure to understand and obey natural forces.

However, the Christian conscience can scarcely be satisfied with this view. THE AVERAGE CHRISTIAN MAN OR WOMAN SPENDS THE GREATER PART OF HIS OR HER WAKING HOURS EARNING A LIVING. Perhaps the longest hours of all are spent by the housewife in her endless tasks of homemaking and child raising. Boys and girls and young people are doing the appointed work of their age level in attending school and studying. Thus for all ages from six to sixty and beyond, the work of the world requires our largest single outlay of time and energy. If this great segment of experience is to be

---

[1] *The Evanston Report* (New York: Harper & Bros., 1955), page 162. Used by permission of the publisher.

removed from the rule of God, then he is not the Lord of all! If we cannot be Christian at work, we are left to obey man rather than God in most of our lives.

MOREOVER, FAILURE TO SEE OUR WORK AS A CHRISTIAN VOCATION TENDS TO DEPRIVE LIFE OF MEANING or to see meaning in the wrong things. Multitudes of workers today engage in a dull routine whose only purpose is the weekly pay check. These are the faces Carl Sandburg saw on the Halsted Street car, "tired of wishes, empty of dreams." At the opposite extreme are those who work with great energy and verve in order to get ahead, earn more money, get promoted, and gain power and prestige. Thus the president of a large electric appliance manufacturing company who was born in a Bronx tenement relates how he was driven by a boyhood dream "to succeed and have a house on the top of a hill."

A metropolitan newspaper tells the story of a sixty-four-year-old sixteen-thousand-dollar-a-year executive who retired a year ahead of time because "he had begun to question the values of his life." He had achieved the financial success he craved but found that he now wanted to be a vice-president. He knew if he became vice-president, he would drive himself to be president.

> I believe a lot of business people are all mixed up in their values. They believe in business success which brings a working man about the only glory he ever gets, and they believe in money. So they strive very hard for both. And the more of both they get the more they realize their hunger can't be satisfied.

Surely there must be something more rewarding in this life than luncheon clubs. There must be something better as a way of life than going away from home 9 to 10 hours a day to toil at a task someone else has designated for you. There must be something better than competing, compromising, and arguing, and always trying to get.[2]

In affirming the importance of work as a proper field of Christian activity, the Second Assembly of the World Council of Churches recognized this possibility of mistaken emphasis. It said:

Though it is right to stress the importance of work as God's ordinance for human life, it happens in some places that an idol is made out of work. Work is not the whole of life, and when men make it their chief object in living, they are prevented from coming into right relationships with God and with their fellow-men.[3]

AGAIN, FAILURE TO SEE THE WORLD OF WORK AS INCLUDED IN THE DOMAIN OF CHRISTIAN SERVICE HAS MADE THE CHRISTIAN FAITH OF MANY SEEM UNREAL AND IRRELEVANT. If God is to be served only in acts of specifically "religious" character—verbal witnessing, hymn singing and Bible reading, acting on church boards and committees—then for most people the opportunities to serve him will be very limited. God will be real to the clergy, because they

---

[2] *Chicago Daily News*, November 11, 1955. Used by permission.
[3] *The Evanston Report*, p. 163.

are continually handling sacred things, but the laity will only occasionally be engaged in God's work. However, if we can feel that our Christian vocation is to serve God not only with witness and worship, but also with the work of our hands and minds, then we will be working with him long hours every day.

MOREOVER THE PERSONAL CONTACTS OF OUR WORKING SITUATION AFFORD MANY OPPORTUNITIES TO SPEAK A WORD FOR CHRIST. The quality of Christian living—the self-control, the kindness and good will, the ready helpfulness and understanding of the Christian—will now as always be a powerful testimony for our Lord. However, the work itself, if it is contributing to the common welfare and meeting the needs of men, can be done as an offering to God.

> While, of course, the Christian layman will miss no suitable occasion for bearing his testimony to the truth, he will regard his job as itself a matter in which he may directly serve his Lord. He will bear witness not only with his lips but by the quality of his workmanship; he will do his work as "unto his Master in heaven." A right understanding of the doctrine of Creation will remind him that God has given to man an awesome capacity to change the face of nature by his work.[4]

This is what George Eliot was saying in her poem about Stradivarius, the great violinmaker. Naldo, a

---

[4] *Ibid.*, page 164.

painter who is thoroughly unprincipled in his work, cannot understand why Stradivarius at sixty-nine still takes so much joy in his work. He says tauntingly:

> 'Tis a petty kind of fame
> At best, that comes of making violins.

But Stradivarius replies that he cares nothing for fame, that his reward will come:

> When any master holds
> 'Twixt chin and hand a violin of mine,
>
> .   .   .   .
>
> The masters only know whose work is good:
> They will choose mine, and while God gives them skill
> I give them instruments to play upon,
> God choosing me to help him.

Naldo argues further, saying that the old workman is mistaken, since others can make violins as good as his. But the violinmaker says that while Giuseppe's violins may be as good, they are different.

> But were his the best,
> He could not work for two. My work is mine.
> And . . . if my hand slacked
> I should rob God— . . .
> Leaving a blank instead of violins.

Is some such feeling as this possible for those who do the world's work today?

II

A CHRISTIAN VIEW OF WORK BEGINS WITH THE RECOGNI-
TION THAT IN HIS CREATIVE ACTIVITY GOD HIMSELF IS A
WORKER. "My Father is working still, and I am working," said Jesus (John 5:17 R.S.V.). God's labor to
create in this corner of his universe a home for his children did not end with the creation story of Genesis. Age
after age, century after century, he maintains, refines, and
perfects his workmanship. Alike in the processes of
nature, the events of history, and the lives of men, the
divine Artisan is seeking to express his purpose with
sweeping stroke and massive plan. Sometimes the Master
Workman's face must be deeply lined, sometimes his
mouth firmly set, as he struggles to master and redeem
the intractable material of our human lives. But always
there is the patient panorama of the centuries.

> We serve no God whose work is done,
>   Who rests within His firmament:
> Our God, His labors but begun
>   Toils evermore, with power unspent.[5]

Then too the Christian remembers that his Master
worked in the Nazareth carpenter shop and knew how
to fashion the yoke which the oxen could bear easily
and lightly. If, as Christianity asserts, the divine nature
was in Christ, then God himself did not hesitate to take

---

[5] Thomas Curtis Clark, "The Faith of Christ's Freemen." Used by permission of
Mrs. Thomas Curtis Clark.

the plane and saw in hand and to strike the nail with the hammer. The work which Jesus knew was not only that of preaching, teaching, and healing, but also that of physical toil. The realization that Jesus was a worker has inspired modern poets to write such hymns as "O Master Workman of the Race" and Milton Littlefield's

> O Son of Man, Thou madest known,
> Through quiet work in shop and home,
> The sacredness of common things,
> The chance of life that each day brings.

Through the centuries Christian leaders and saints have not hesitated to work long, hard hours, with both mind and hand. Many, such as Augustine, Luther, Wesley, came into leadership from the scholar's desk, which is itself an arduous form of toil. But many others have known hard physical labor. Paul on his missionary journeys supported himself by working at his trade as a tentmaker. Francis of Assisi began the road to sainthood by selling his silks and satins and laboring with his own hands to rebuild a ruined church. John Bunyan was a tinker and William Carey a cobbler. And of course the unknown and unsung rank and file who make up the great body of the Church's "mighty army" have always been drawn from those who toil. *Far from feeling that work is a curse to be avoided, Christians think that their work is a challenge to share with God in his task of creation.* This is the first plank in a Christian doctrine of work.

A SECOND CONVICTION IS THAT EACH CHRISTIAN HAS A VOCATION OR CALL (LATIN: VOCARE—TO CALL), OBEDIENCE TO WHICH SETS THE ARENA IN WHICH HE WILL DO GOD'S WILL IN DAILY WORK. Paul develops this idea in writing to his converts at Corinth (I Corinthians 7:17-24). In part this call of God is set for us in the conditions of our birth. We come into the world male or female, white or colored, American or foreigner. (For Paul the equivalents were Jew or Gentile, bond or free.) We can do nothing about these factors. Their glad acceptance is part of our faithful obedience to God. Each of us also has his unique endowment of talents and abilities. There are some things we can do and some that we cannot. So far as our lifework is determined by these given factors of birth and ability, we do not choose our tasks, we accept them.

However, there is also a large area of choice in which we are left to discover what God's will for us may be. Our society offers more freedom of movement to the individual than did Paul's. We do not have to stay on the side of the tracks where we were born! But even Paul advised slaves to avail themselves of the opportunity of becoming free if it should offer itself. If I have more than one talent, which one represents God's purpose for my life? If several jobs are available, which shall I take? It has been said that "where my abilities meet the needs of the world, that is God's will for my life." But if there are several needs which I might serve, which do I answer? In such matters the Christian is responsible for rightly reading the purpose of God.

The point to remember is that in any Christian teaching about work vocation or call must not be confined to specifically "religious" professions such as the ministry, missionary service, and the like. *There is a Christian call to be a carpenter, farmer, steel worker, or housewife no less than to preach, teach, or nurse.* If the historic Protestant doctrine of "the priesthood of all believers" means anything, it must mean that laymen are expected to serve God in their work just as ministers serve God in theirs.

Does this mean that *any* secular occupation is an appropriate one for the Christian? It would seem obvious *that some occupations might be so negative and destructive in their effects as to be clearly unsuitable for a Christian, but it is often difficult to draw the line of demarcation.* That is why many Christian scientists, for example, have tortured consciences in these days. Research which unlocks the secrets of the universe is good—it puts new possibilities for the enrichment of life at man's disposal. But it also has potential for the destruction of life, and this is bad. What shall the nuclear scientist who is also a Christian do? Or consider the plight of the advertising man. Modern business depends upon the large volume distribution of goods made possible by mass advertising. But suppose the product is useless or even harmful, and suppose its sale demands a campaign of misrepresentation and spurious claims. Will the Christian stay out of advertising altogether or refuse to take part in campaigns that violate his conscience? If he is a manager or owner of an agency, doubtless he can refuse certain commissions, but has an employee similar freedom of action?

The Second Assembly of the World Council of Churches made certain suggestions to help Christians with decisions of this kind. The report of the commission on the laity said this in part:

> (a) Work is the necessary ordering of daily life so that human needs may be fulfilled and as such work begins every morning in farm, factory and home. . . . Earthly success will not be the highest standard by which Christians judge their daily work. While they will want to insist that work receives a decent and just recompense, adequate for the worker and his dependents, Christians yet know that, whatever may be its reward in this life, their labour is not in vain in the Lord. . . .

> (b) All honest work is service rendered to society. . . . When [this truth] is ignored and men think only of their rights and not of the services which they may render to the community, they violate their own nature; increased production or higher rewards become ends in themselves. . . . The relevance of the Christian teaching about service to one's neighbour is obvious here. Every human being, worthy or unworthy, becomes one's neighbour, and the Christian rejoices that in his work he may thus, however feebly, reflect the goodness of God, who causes His sun to shine and his rain to fall on the just and the unjust alike.

> (c) Implanted in all men is a desire to create new forms of being and of value, and it is in the work

of the very few that this power of creation is seen at the highest level. . . . Man's spontaneous joy in the creative element in work is a sign of that freedom for which creation longs and of the truth that man shall subdue the earth and have dominion over it.[6]

III

What does all this mean for the individual Christian? Have any principles emerged from the foregoing discussion to help the Christian decide what work he will do and how he will conduct himself in the world of work? Let us begin by asking how the sincere Christian who earnestly desires to obey God's will for his life can find the work he ought to do.

1. CHRISTIAN VOCATIONAL DECISION BEGINS WITH SELF-UNDERSTANDING. What are the conditions of life into which I have been born? Does my mental, physical, or emotional nature indicate what doors are open or closed to me? For example, a woman may well feel that the very fact of her womanhood indicates homemaking, wifehood, and motherhood as her Christian vocation. Even if under modern conditions she may enter the economic world, she may well think of this as a tentative and temporary condition. Of course many women do not marry, and others have such special gifts that they combine career and marriage. For such the problems of Christian vocational choice are the same as for men.

---

[6] *The Evanston Report*, pages 164-65. Used by permission of Harper & Bros.

2. INCLUDED IN SELF-UNDERSTANDING IS THE MATTER OF RIGHTLY APPRAISING ONE'S TALENTS AND ABILITIES. What are my aptitudes and interests? In what subjects did I do best at school? Do I have mechanical ingenuity and skill? Am I fascinated by ideas and the world of books? Do I like laboratory work so that I should consider a life of research? Have I patience with children, and do I enjoy working with them so that I ought to teach? Do I like to see things grow, and do I enjoy working with animals? Today there are many aptitude tests which can give help in this matter of self-understanding, and most school systems have some kind of vocational guidance program to help young people discover what occupations they are best suited for.

3. WHAT ARE THE NEEDS OF THE WORLD? The Christian will not be satisfied merely to find work that gives him the satisfactions of self-expression and the financial means of maintaining life. Work must also be socially useful, it must serve the community, enrich the lives of others, provide the necessities of our human existence— not only physical but mental, emotional, and spiritual. It is in this sense that one might scrub floors no less than write a book "for the glory of God."

In our land of crop surpluses and of ability to produce more than we can buy, it is sometimes hard to remember that the world as a whole is still in desperate need of adequate food, clothing, and shelter. Some Christians may well feel that God's call to them is to participate in programs such as Point IV projects to increase the productivity of underdeveloped regions. Others may accept a vocation to find ways to solve the perplexing problems of distribution which periodically shut down our factories while there are still unmet needs to supply.

Any discussion of the world's needs would be inadequate from a Christian point of view which did not recognize that our deepest needs are intangible and spiritual. We need an understanding of life's meaning more than we need our next meal. We need to feel that we are significant and important in the eternal scheme of things more than we need a new suit. We need a worthy cause to serve with our lives more than we need social security for our lives. Such an understanding of the world's needs will lead many, not into the production of goods, but into one of the many service vocations which are open today.

4. THIS LEADS TO WHAT HAS TRADITIONALLY BEEN REGARDED AS SPECIFICALLY RELIGIOUS VOCATION—THE MINISTRY, MISSIONARY SERVICE, CHRISTIAN TEACHING, AND THE LIKE. The view I have been urging is that all useful work offers a potentially Christian vocation—if it is performed "for the glory of God and the service of man." This is an important and needed emphasis. However, it must not dull the fact that the world and the Church are in desperate need of dedicated men and women who will confront our age with the good news of the gospel of Christ.

One denomination alone (the Methodist) estimates that it needs twelve hundred young men and women for its ministry each year merely to replace those who die and retire. It needs an additional sixteen hundred to provide the expansion which our rapidly growing population demands and the opportunities of evangelization present. This number is needed for the pastoral ministry alone, to say nothing of the needs for missionaries, teachers for Christian schools and colleges, social workers, campus leadership, chaplaincies, and many other forms of specialized service. *If a Christian young man or woman possessed the personal gifts and abilities to perform one of these tasks which the world needs so urgently, but settled for being a salesman or professional person because these also are Christian vocations, would not this be a violation of the will of God?*

The advice of an older minister to a young man has often been quoted with approval: "Do not go into the ministry if you can keep out of it." An important fact is meant here: namely, that there should be a sense of divine compulsion in the decision to enter the ministry. However, it cannot be doubted that this advice has kept many out of the Christian ministry who should have entered it. If a young person is sincerely Christian and concerned to know God's will for his or her life, why should he not consider full-time Christian service first instead of last? Appraising his abilities and the world's needs, why should he not ask first, Is there some place in full-time church-related service that my unique gifts can meet the world's needs? Only if he is sure that the answer to the above question is No will he consider what else God's purpose for his life may be.

IV

So far we have considered why it is important to see the world of work in relation to God's will and what a Christian doctrine of work might be. We have tried to formulate some principles which might guide the Christian in the selection of his lifework. There remains to ask what guidance the Christian faith can provide for the performance of the task once it has been chosen.

1. First of all the Christian will be sure of his vocation. He will not be satisfied to drift into some occupation by mere chance. It may be that he will find himself in some work which he entered before he took his religious confession seriously and which he now feels does not permit him to serve God and man. If so, he will begin at once to re-examine his gifts and the world's needs. If this compels him to leave a line of work he has come to feel is unchristian—or at least not God's will for him—he will be sustained by the knowledge that he is doing God's will.

2. Being sure of his vocation, the Christian will have a changed attitude toward his work. He sees what he is doing as a part of God's purpose; therefore it has dignity and meaning. He does not do his work grudgingly or as drudgery. Rather he finds joy and satisfaction in his work. Christian faith makes a man sober, industrious, dependable; therefore he becomes a better worker. He will not knowingly defraud any man; consequently he gives an honest day's work for a day's pay. In short, the Christian worker is a good worker.

3. A CHRISTIAN HAS A DIFFERENT ATTITUDE TOWARD HIS FELLOW WORKERS. Few jobs are done in solitude. Even the man who tills a one-family farm is involved with his neighbors, with members of his co-op, with those to whom he sells or from whom he buys. The Christian sees his fellow worker not as a rival for advancement, but as another child of God. Important as the work may be, the worker is more important. The interpersonal relations of factory, farm, or market place present opportunities to display to our fellows the same concern and good will that we have experienced in God's dealings with us.

4. THE CHRISTIAN'S ATTITUDE TOWARD HIS EMPLOYER IS ALSO CHANGED. Actually, he regards those in positions of authority over him as fellow workers. Employer and employee, owner, management, and laborer are distinctions of task, not of status. When work is seen in relation to God, our human differences are insignificant. All of us are workers at God's tasks. The Christian worker is neither subservient to his superior nor overbearing to his subordinate. He sees all alike as mortal men who stand in need of God's grace.

5. THE CHRISTIAN WORKER WILL BE A RESPONSIBLE PARTICIPANT IN WHATEVER ORGANIZATIONS ARE APPROPRIATE FOR HIS OCCUPATION. He will not be a "lone wolf," seeking only his own welfare and indifferent to his fellows. If he belongs to a labor union, he will attend meetings, take part in discussions of policy, and use his influence for Christian decisions which take account of *all* interests— owners and consumers, as well as workers. If he belongs

to a trade association, he will be on the side of fair prices and wages, good working conditions, honest advertising, and public responsibility.

> The goal of industrial relations still remains the development of mutual understanding, confidence, and respect between management and employees. There is no more important responsibility of management than the promotion of sound human relations. This is so because the human being is the indispensable ingredient of business.[7]

6. THE CHRISTIAN WORKER WILL HAVE A DIFFERENT SET OF VALUES. Of course he will want to provide what is necessary for his wife and children, but he will know that not nearly so much is required for a good life as the world thinks. He knows that the important question about a job is not "How much does it pay?" but "How useful is it?" Because he knows himself to be a child of God, he does not need a house on the best street and two cars in the garage in order to feel important.

It was John Wesley's custom to preach each morning at 5 o'clock to workers on their way to ten, twelve, even fourteen hours of hard, often unattractive toil. A writer pictures them going to work from these services:

> . . . walking, often before sunrise, the cobbled streets of the town, the rough country roads and the slag-strewn paths of industrial and mining districts, and

---

[7] From an address, "The Responsibility of Management," by James F. Oates, Jr., published by the Men's Club of the First Methodist Church, Evanston, Ill.

singing on their way the hymns that Charles Wesley had written for them:

> Forth in thy name, O Lord, I go
>   My daily labour to pursue;
> Thee, only Thee, resolved to know,
>   In all I think or speak or do.[8]

Could this hymn express the attitude of present-day Christians on their way to work?

FOR THOUGHT AND DISCUSSION

Scripture background: Read I Corinthians 7:17-24. Also John 5:17; Mark 10:42-45; I Thessalonians 4:9-12; II Thessalonians 3:6-13. On the basis of these and any other passages that may occur to you, can you formulate a Christian doctrine of work?

Construct a check list of questions which a Christian might use to help him decide whether a specific occupation offered him a Christian vocation.

Do you agree that there are given factors of birth which constitute a state into which we are called of God? What does this mean for lifework?

What is the program of vocational guidance in the schools of your community? Are religious vocations included among those recommended to young people?

How do the needs of the world affect the Christian's

---

[8] W. L. Doughty, *John Wesley, Preacher* (London: Epworth Press, 1955), page 171. For other stanzas of this hymn see *The Methodist Hymnal*, No. 290.

vocational decision? How do we know what those needs are? What do you think are some of the most urgent?

What are some of the moral problems that confront Christians in the occupations most commonly followed in your community? What help is available for their solution?

CHAPTER 8

Being Christian With Money

IT IS STARTLING TO DISCOVER HOW MUCH OF THE TEACHING
of Jesus is devoted to the subject of the right use of
wealth. We think of Jesus as the master of the spiritual
life but find him talking again and again about material
things. Some authorities estimate that as much as one
half of his recorded teaching has to do with some aspect
of our attitude toward money. If Jesus saw wealth as
one of the great problems in the spiritual life, we can
scarcely conclude a study of what it means to be a
Christian without giving attention to the subject.

In his great first book, *The Christ of the Indian Road*,
E. Stanley Jones told of the conversion of the Saxons
who

> were practically compelled [by Charlemagne] to
> become Christians. They consented on one condi-
> tion. That condition would only be known at the
> time of their baptism. When these warriors were
> put under the water as a symbol that their old life
> was dead, they went under—all except their right

arms. They held them out, lifted above their heads. These were their fighting arms. They were never Christianized! [1]

When we consider the high value our civilization places on wealth, we are compelled to wonder if modern man has not also held his right arm out of the water—and in his hand a tightly clasped pocketbook!

I

What then is a Christian attitude toward wealth?

1. JESUS DID NOT REGARD THE MATERIAL WORLD AS IN ITSELF EVIL. He bewildered many of his contemporaries by not fitting into the ascetic pattern of a John the Baptist, for he came "eating and drinking." He accepted the invitations and the support of wealthy friends and commended a woman who anointed him with costly ointment. Christianity has been rightly classified as "a world-affirming religion."

2. IT IS NOT MONEY BUT THE LOVE OF MONEY THAT IS "THE ROOT OF ALL EVIL" (I Timothy 6:10). It is a matter of proportion and relative values. The successful farmer was criticized not for raising bumper crops, but for supposing that they provided security for his soul (Luke 12:13-21). The rich young ruler was condemned not for being wealthy, but for valuing his wealth before the kingdom of God (Mark 10:17-22). In our hearts we know that the love of money cannot satisfy our deepest

---

[1] Page 12.

longings, yet the things that money will buy become so important to us that we let them crowd out the things that money cannot buy.

> Many a man today who has "great possessions" knows in his heart that financial success is not enough: he has just about everything that anyone could dream of—except happiness, peace of mind, and the feeling that he has done something worthwhile with his life.[2]

3. MONEY (MAMMON) IS THE GREAT RIVAL OF GOD FOR MAN'S AFFECTIONS (MATTHEW 6:24). Milton in *Paradise Lost* describes this archrival as:

... the least erected spirit that fell
From heaven; for ev'n in heaven his looks and thoughts
Were always downward bent, admiring more
The riches of heaven's pavement, trodden gold,
Than aught divine or holy else enjoy'd
In vision beatific.

After the young ruler went away sorrowing, Jesus commented upon the difficulty of a wealthy person entering the Kingdom (Mark 10:23-31). Eighteen centuries later John Wesley remarked: "I have not known threescore rich persons, perhaps not half the number, during three-score years, who, as far as I can judge, were not less holy than they would have been had they been

---

[2] Ernest F. Tittle, *The Gospel According to Luke* (New York: Harper & Bros., 1951), page 137. Used by permission of the publisher.

poor." [3] And again: "The Methodists grow more and more self-indulgent, because they *grow rich.* . . . And it is an observation which admits of few exceptions, that nine in ten of these decreased in grace, in the same proportion as they increased in wealth." [4]

4. UNDUE ANXIETY ABOUT OUR PHYSICAL NEEDS SHOWS A LACK OF FAITH IN GOD'S PROVIDENCE (MATTHEW 6:25-34). The birds of the air and the flowers of the field are fed and clothed; God certainly cares more for us. Pagans spend their greatest energies accumulating food and clothing, as if life consisted in the abundance of things we possess! But Christians are to trust God for these needs and seek first God's kingdom and his righteousness and these other things will be added as well.

Now this is certainly not an invitation to a life of sloth and idleness. Paul had to write to a church which misunderstood this basic Christian teaching, "If any one will not work, let him not eat" (II Thessalonians 3:10 R.S.V.). Neither is this a counsel of improvidence. As Dr. Ernest F. Tittle reminds us:

> Jesus does not belittle the material; we are to pray for daily bread as well as for forgiveness. He does not decry working, saving, looking ahead, the absence of which simply means that others will have to look out for us or our families. What is here deplored is a life that magnifies the material and neglects God.[5]

---

[3] From Sermon LXVIII: "The Wisdom of God's Counsels."
[4] From Sermon CXVI: "Causes of the Inefficacy of Christianity."
[5] *Op. cit.*, page 137.

Again it is a matter of proportion. We certainly have an obligation to meet the responsibilities of supporting our families, but we have no obligation to provide them the most luxurious quarters in town. We do not have to demonstrate the worth of our characters—nor can we—by achieving a big bank balance. To be overanxious about material things is to doubt that God has planned a world where there is enough for all his children and to distract our attention from doing his will.

5. THE LAST THING TO SAY ABOUT A CHRISTIAN ATTITUDE TOWARD MONEY IS THAT MAN IS TO BE GENEROUS WITH HIS WEALTH AS GOD IS GENEROUS WITH US. God is the householder who pays the laborers in his vineyard not according to a strict accounting of hours and wage rates, but according to their willingness and need (Matthew 20:1-16). The Samaritan who responded to the need of the wounded man beside the road and from his own purse paid for his lodging and care is commended as the example of one who loved neighbor as self (Luke 10:29-37). The God who pours out his good gifts upon both the just and the unjust is the perfect example whom we are called to emulate.

II

What it means to be Christian with money might be discussed under three divisions: earning money, using money, and giving money. FIRST, THEN, WHAT CAN BE SAID ABOUT A CHRISTIAN'S EARNING OF MONEY? Something has already been implied about this in the discussion of the Christian's choice of vocation. However, we need to look at it more specifically.

One of the classic discussions of wealth in Christian literature is a sermon by John Wesley on "The Use of Money." He preached on this subject many times[6] and thought it so important that he included the sermon among the forty-four Standard Sermons that he published for the doctrinal guidance of the Methodist societies. It is in this sermon that he gave the famous advice: "Gain all you can. . . . save all you can. . . . Give all you can."

It is evident at once that any advice to Christians to "gain all [they] can" is subject to certain qualifications. For one thing, they will not, as Wesley put it, buy "gold too dear, without paying more for it than it is worth." Occupations which endanger the worker's health or life will be scrutinized to see if the product is worth the precious risk. Employment which requires a violation of either the legal or the moral code will be refused. Other occupations endanger our neighbors either in soul or in bodies. Here Wesley speaks specifically of the sale of "spirituous liquors." "All who sell them in the common way, to any that will buy," he says, "are poisoners general. They murder His Majesty's subjects by wholesale, neither does their eye pity or spare." [7]

Assuming that the Christian is engaged in an occupa-

---

[6] First preached in 1744, the sermon was repeated in 1748, seven times in 1750, five times in 1751, six times in 1752, twice in 1753, once in 1757. It was first published in 1760. It now appears as Sermon XLIV in the *Standard Sermons, Volume II.*
[7] *Ibid.*, page 318.

tion that avoids these negative aspects and can be followed as a constructive contribution to the common good, *he will apply himself with industry, diligence, and imagination.*

> Gain all you can, by common sense, by using in your business all the understanding which God has given you. . . . You should be continually learning, from the experience of others, or from your own experience, reading, and reflection, to do everything you have to do better to-day than you did yesterday.[8]

If this advice seems to the modern reader to sanction an unbridled pursuit of wealth, let him remember the restrictions that surround the getting and the subsequent admonition to "give all you can." It is a *Christian* who is gaining all he can. He will, of course, engage in no dishonest dealings. There will be no covetousness, no sharp practices, no lying misrepresentations. *Caveat emptor,* let the buyer beware, will not be the accepted rule of his business. Further, the Christian earner will never let the love of money replace the love of God in his affections. This will be both achieved and evidenced by his giving all he can.

III

The Christian is concerned not only with how he earns his money, but also with how he uses it. Here Mr.

---

[8] *Ibid.*, page 320.

Wesley's advice is, "Save all you can." This implies in the first place a counsel to simple and frugal living. The Christian will not indulge in luxury and ostentation. Self-indulgence and pride are the two sins to be avoided here.

As a family's income increases, it is a natural desire to provide more adequate housing, clothing, and food for them. Up to the point of meeting the necessities of life, this is a legitimate purpose. *However, the Christian lives under the command to love his neighbor as himself, and he has been told that any human being in need is his neighbor.* We know the poverty and limitations under which vast numbers of our fellows live in overpopulated, underdeveloped parts of the world, in displaced persons camps, in famine or flood areas. In the face of such needs, the Christian cannot in good conscience engage in extravagant and needless expenditure. In order to be a good neighbor, he will limit himself to a simple style of life and will "save all [he] can."

Again, the matter of sinful pride is involved in our use of money. The economist Thorstein Veblen used to speak of "conspicuous consumption," by which he meant purchases which were not really necessary, but were intended to impress the neighbors. A bigger house than any other in town, on the most exclusive street, with two or three cars—these are not things I need except as badges of how successful I am. *Such expenditures feed my pride, but they separate me from God.*

A recent study[9] of the spending habits of urban families in America revealed that the average budget looked like this:

% OF TOTAL	ITEM	TOTAL EXPENDED
29.1	Food	$1,309.50
25.2	Housing	1,134.00
5.4	Furniture	243.00
12.2	Clothing	549.00
10.9	Transportation	490.50
4.4	Medical	198.00
6.6	Recreation	297.00
6.2	Miscellaneous (Including insurance—$152, gifts, savings, etc.)	279.00
	Total expended	$4,500.00
	Taxes withheld	560.00
	Total earnings	$5,060.00

This average Mr. and Mrs. Jones are thirty and twenty-seven years old, have been married four years, have one child with a second expected. They live in a five-room house which cost them $10,500 and on which they still owe about $7,000.

A representative young couple with six children on a 330-acre one-family farm in New Hampshire reported

---

[9] Clair Huffaker, "Meet the Joneses." Reprinted from *This Week* magazine. Copyright 1956 by the United Newspapers Magazine Corporation.

their finances to a national magazine.[10] They grossed $13,656 from their dairy farm, and their annual costs of operation were $11,892. This left them $1,764, or $147 a month for living expenses. Their budget was as follows:

Food (staples not raised on farm)	$ 38.00
Clothing	6.00
Electricity and phone	7.75
Insurance (home and life)	28.90
Medical	16.10
Recreation	1.00
Church and charities	15.00
Car expenses	7.00
Freezer-locker and meat packaging	5.00
Household supplies	4.00
Children's school expense	8.00
Club dues	.50
Publications	1.75
Small unexpected outgo	8.00
	$147.00

How do these family budgets compare with the expenditures of the average family in your community? How do they compare with your own? How do the urban and rural families compare with each other? Can you make any criticism from a Christian point of view of the distribution of funds among these items?

---

[10] "Be Happy Here," *Ladies' Home Journal*, December, 1956. Reprinted by special permission of the *Ladies' Home Journal*. Copyright 1956 by The Curtis Publishing Company.

Dr. Arthur E. Morgan in a commencement address at Antioch College, Ohio, some years ago gave an interesting example of the significance for Christian character of the spending habits of working young people:

> Two men . . . were employed by a certain corporation as accountants, each on a salary of five thousand dollars a year. One of them selected for himself a standard of living that required him to spend every dollar he made. He postponed the having of children but not of an expensive automobile, a golf club membership, a membership in a club in the city. The other man lived on a two-acre tract out of town. He and his wife and children got most of their exercise in the garden. A three-year-old automobile furnished transportation. They found books and magazines to be cheaper than musical comedies. They found considerable exploration necessary in order to build up a supply of friends with tastes similar to their own but still economically within their reach. A quarter of their income went into savings. Came a day when the corporation these men worked for got into serious financial difficulties through dishonest management and they were ordered to falsify their accounts. One of them refused—not the one who had lived up every dollar he made. He, poor fellow, capitulated, lacking the courage to face economic disaster and the loss of luxuries on which he had allowed himself to become dependent.[11]

---

[11] Related by Tittle, *op. cit.*, pages 139-40.

Dr. Morgan's comment is, "Idealism is most effective when it has paid its price in advance, when the crisis finds it ready, tempered to hard and simple living, with its resources turned into reserves and not consumed by current wants."

IV

THE WESLEYAN ADVICE TO "GAIN ALL YOU CAN . . . SAVE ALL YOU CAN" IS NOT COMPLETE UNLESS THE THIRD ADMONITION IS ADDED—"GIVE ALL YOU CAN." At this point Mr. Wesley practiced what he preached. In 1738 he hit upon the idea of publishing inexpensive books and tracts. As he became famous, many of these had a very large sale and, as he said, "made me rich in spite of myself." All that was produced beyond what was required to maintain the business and to provide his simple wants was given away. In his latter years it is estimated that he gave away a thousand pounds a year and about thirty thousand pounds in his lifetime. He used to say that men could call him "a thief and a liar" if he died possessed of more than ten pounds. At his death beyond the publishing business he had only the loose change in his pockets and six pounds he had provided for the men who carried him to his grave.

THE CHRISTIAN'S GIVING SPRINGS FROM THE RECOGNITION THAT ALL THINGS ARE GOD'S; MAN IS ONLY A STEWARD, A TRUSTEE. "The earth is the Lord's, and the fulness thereof." As they place their gifts on the altar, God's people sing:

115

We give Thee but Thine own,
    Whate'er the gift may be:
All that we have is Thine alone,
    A trust, O Lord, from Thee.

We know how scrupulously a trustee of a church or trust fund is expected to use the resources entrusted to him not for his own benefit, but for the purpose of the donor. Are we as careful to use the resources God has given us for his work?

CHRISTIAN GIVING ALSO IS DERIVED FROM THE CHARACTER OF GOD. The God and Father of our Lord Jesus Christ is a self-giving God. We cannot come into full communion with him until we share his nature by our own self-giving. This is why Jesus commended the widow who cast "all her living" into the temple treasury. The infant churches in Greece were composed of people for the most part of meager resources who scarcely had enough for their own needs, yet when Paul told them of the suffering of the church in Jerusalem, they gave a generous offering (II Corinthians 9). When John Wesley first preached his sermon on "The Use of Money," his London congregation of poor people responded with an offering of fifty pounds, so that he was able "within the hour" to buy clothing and shoes for many needy and deserving families. So it has always been. Christians give because God has so richly given to them.

HOW MUCH SHOULD A CHRISTIAN GIVE? "Give all you can" was Wesley's answer.

If you desire to be a faithful and a wise steward, out of that portion of your Lord's goods which He has for the present lodged in your hands, . . . first, provide things needful for yourself; food to eat, raiment to put on, whatever nature moderately requires for preserving the body in health and strength. Secondly, provide these for your wife, your children, your servants, or any others who pertain to your household. If, when this is done, there be an overplus left, then "do good to them that are of the household of faith." If there be an overplus still, "as you have opportunity, do good unto all men." In so doing, you give all you can; nay, in a sound sense, all you have.[12]

There has been much discussion of the Old Testament tithe as a standard of giving that is authoritative for the Christian. Some hold that this is a practice adapted to a simple agricultural economy where the crop can be tithed at harvest time, but one that cannot and should not be applied to an industrial economy where weekly or monthly wages are for many barely adequate for a minimum living standard. Others say that Jesus approved the tithe when he said to those who carried tithing so far that they even set aside a tenth of the herbs used in cooking: "These you ought to have done without neglecting the others" (Matthew 23:23b R.S.V.).

Here are two examples that may help you reach your own decision on the important question, How much should a Christian give?

---

[12] Op. cit., page 324.

My own experience after trying many ways is that the biblical tithe serves well as the basic regular portion. There need be no legalism about such giving if it is as a man has purposed in his heart. To be sure, the 10 per cent looms larger the smaller the income, and there is no real justice about the question. Nevertheless, this part of our income is possible. . . . With a tithe for a basis we can always give more on special occasions of thanksgiving or when particular needs call for our help.[13]

In an obscure valley of southeastern France in the eighteenth century John Frederic Oberlin achieved an amazing career as village pastor, educator, agricultural pioneer, and philanthropist. Out of his meager salary he managed to support his own large family, give generously to the church, finance many pioneer projects for which there was no other support, and help the poor. The financial plan by which he achieved this has been described as follows:

He felt now that some of his capacity for doing good was also going to waste through lack of the application of a more rigorous and exact system to his benefactions. So, to avoid future loss through lack of system in deposits and accounting, Oberlin made himself three boxes.

In the first box he deposited one-tenth of his earnings as a gift for maintaining public worship. In the second box he deposited another tenth of his

---

[13] Nels Ferre, *Making Religion Real* (New York: Harper & Bros., 1955), pages 132-33. Used by permission of the publisher.

earnings, as a source of gifts toward community improvements, prizes for school children, entertaining strangers, redressing injuries done to any person by malefactors in his parish, and for other purposes. The contents of the third box, in which he deposited the third tenth of his income, were to be used for the poor.[14]

Someone has called money "minted life." It represents so many minutes, hours, or days of our life's energy. What will we buy with it?

FOR THOUGHT AND DISCUSSION

Bible background: Make a list of all the incidents and teachings you can recall where Jesus deals with the subject of wealth or money. Can all these be classified under one or another of the principles discussed in Section I? Be sure your list includes at least the various passages referred to in the text.

What do you think of the principles suggested in Section I for a Christian attitude toward wealth? Do you disagree with any? Would you change any of the statements or add others in the light of your understanding of the teaching of Jesus?

What do you understand Jesus to mean by the command, "Do not be anxious, saying, 'What shall we eat?' or 'What shall we drink?' or 'What shall we wear?'" (Matthew 6:31 R.S.V.)?

---

[14] Marshall Dawson, *Oberlin, a Protestant Saint* (New York: Willett, Clark & Co., 1934), page 78. Used by permission of Harper & Bros.

Is it dangerous to advise people to "gain all [they] can"? What restrictions will a Christian place upon his earnings? Can you think of some specific ways in which a Christian should not earn money?

Make a list of principles which would guide a Christian in spending his money. In what ways does "keeping up with the Joneses" involve us in unnecessary expense?

Can you construct a budget for an average income family in your community which would provide for their legitimate needs and also for Christian generosity? How does your personal budget compare with this?

What biblical teachings can you recall which might guide a Christian in his giving?

What are the arguments for and against the tithe as a standard for Christians?

Bishop Ralph S. Cushman has said: "Most people do not give enough to keep their souls alive." What do you think he means by this? Do you agree?

CHAPTER 9

To Be Christian
Do We Need the Church?

BASED ON A POLL OF HARVARD AND RADCLIFFE UNDERGRADU-
ates, a well-known psychologist makes the following
generalizations:

1. Most students feel the need of including a
religious sentiment somewhere within their matur-
ing personalities;

2. For the most part they believe in a God,
though their view is not usually of the traditional
theistic variety;

3. A bare quarter are in essential matters ortho-
dox and historically faithful to theological dogma;

4. The majority maintain some of the forms of
traditional religious practices including prayer;

5. But the majority are clearly dissatisfied with
institutional religion as it exists, so much so that
40 per cent of those who feel a religious need yet
repudiate the church in which they were reared.[1]

---

[1] Gordon Allport, *The Individual and His Religion* (New York: The Macmillan
Co., 1950), page 44. Used by permission of the publisher.

If these statements represent the attitudes of present-day youth, it would seem that more of them are willing to be religious than are concerned to be Christian, and that of those who think of themselves as Christian many, if not most, are dissatisfied with the traditional church as the vehicle for expressing their religious life. Obviously if we wish only to be religious, this can be managed without the Christian Church. But it does seem fair to ask: If we want to be Christian, can we do so without the Church?

Apparently many people think so. Every pastor hears to the point of weariness variations on the theme: "Why should I join the church? I have no need of the church. I am just as good without it as most of the people in it. In fact, by attending church most people pretend to be better than they are. At least I am not a hypocrite!"

I

IS THERE SUCH A THING AS A SOLITARY CHRISTIAN? Is it possible to lead anything resembling a Christian life without active participation in the life of the Christian community, the Church?

In the early days of Christianity under the influence of Eastern asceticism it was thought that a special degree of holiness could be attained by living as a hermit. However, this cannot be accepted as God's intended plan for life, for if everyone followed it, the human race would end. Further, by withdrawing from the world, the hermit makes no contribution to the world. Even in

Roman Catholic practice today those who wish to withdraw from the world gather together in monastic communities to give mutual support to one another.

However, the Protestant who says he can be a Christian without the Church does not stay outside in order to have more time for meditation and so that he can live exclusively unto God as the Roman Catholic recluse intends to do. Rather, he lives in the world, absorbed with worldly and secular concerns and supposes he can keep his soul sensitively alive. He deprives himself of periods of worship and of the support of fellow Christians. He never hears sermons which might help him discover some new word of God for our day. He considers the Church weak and ineffective, but never thinks that it may be so because he and others like him do not give it their support. He professes to live a praiseworthy moral life while separated from the institution which gave the world—and continues to nurture—the very moral standards he accepts.

The man who tries to be a Christian outside the Church is like a man who wishes to have the joys of family life and yet refuses to undertake the responsibilities of marriage. Or to use Elton Trueblood's striking metaphor, he is like a cut flower which can remain healthy in its vase a little time but separated from its roots, finally withers and dies.

THE BIBLE KNOWS NOTHING OF VITAL RELIGIOUS LIFE APART FROM THE COMMUNITY WHICH NURTURES IT. The Old Testament faith is through and through social in its conception of common worship and holy living owed by the nation to its God. The New Testament shows us groups of Christians meeting in upper rooms and in private homes, but always meeting together for prayer and worship. Barnabas and Paul were not free-lance preachers; they were sent on their missionary journeys by the church at Antioch. When disagreement arose as to some implications of the new faith, each individual Christian did not set himself up as an authority, but a church council was summoned and a group decision was reached. There seems to be no warrant in either history or experience for the idea that one can be a Christian outside the Church, any more than one can be a human being outside of human society. *If we want to be Christian, we need the Church.*

II

But what is the Church? Here is an apparently simple question that has caused endless contention among Christians. Disagreement as to the nature of the Church divided Christendom into its three main branches—Eastern, Roman, and Protestant—and separates American Protestantism into more than 250 sects. We will not settle this vexed question here, but perhaps it may be clarified a little.

Obviously the Church is not the structure at Main and Elm, for the Church can exist without buildings. It survived in the catacombs and came out of the rubble of World War II more vital than before. The Church must not be thought of as a social club of congenial people, although often it seems little more. At its best the Church surmounts all differences of culture, race, and social class. Neither is the Church an ethical culture or moral improvement association. Christian morality is the fruit of the Church, not its roots.

What then is the Church?

1. FIRST OF ALL, IT IS A FELLOWSHIP. Its life inheres not in its buildings, organizations, and institutions, but in its people. The Church includes people of many differing backgrounds, but they are unified by their common loyalty to Christ. "By this," Jesus said, "all men will know that you are my disciples, if you have love for one another" (John 13:38 R.S.V.). This warmth of mutual affection makes the Church a fellowship in which the weak are sustained, the mourners are comforted, the tempted are strengthened, and the fallen are lifted up. Children are led tenderly into right paths, youth are challenged to dedicated living, adults find encouragement for the heat of the day, and the old are held in love.

> From hand to hand the greeting flows,
>   From eye to eye the signals run,
> From heart to heart the bright hope glows,
>   The seekers of the Light are one.[2]

2. BUT THE CHURCH IS MORE THAN A FELLOWSHIP; IT IS A FELLOWSHIP OF BELIEVERS. This is what distinguishes the Church from a social club or an ethical society. The

---

[2] Samuel Longfellow.

Church believes that in Christ God has visited and redeemed his people. A fellowship group which does not hold this faith is not a Christian church. The Church also believes that it is not a merely human institution. It did not found itself in the way that a group of men in Independence Hall founded our country. The Church began with a group of men and women waiting in an upper room in Jerusalem for God's action. "You did not choose me, but I chose you" (John 15:16a R.S.V.).

If any man holds the faith of the Church, he is of the Church regardless of his cultural, social, or racial background. A new Christian convert in Asia or Africa and a sophisticated Christian from Europe or America hold more significant things in common than either holds with his non-Christian neighbors. That is why the Festival of Faith which inaugurated the Second Assembly of the World Council of Churches before 125,000 people in Chicago was such a thrilling experience for all who witnessed it. Here was a visible demonstration that the Church brings together people of common faith from every corner of the world into a fellowship of believers.

> Which is the true Church? . . . Let us go back to *New Testament* times for the answer. The Christian Church in *Acts* and in the *Epistles* of Paul was a very simple church when compared to our elaborate organizations today. It was a fellowship, not just an organization or institution. It was a fellowship of faith, the faith that God had come to

men in Christ. Wherever that faith is found today, we have a true church.[3]

3. As A FELLOWSHIP OF BELIEVERS THE CHURCH IS THE BODY OF CHRIST. This stimulating phrase of Paul's has become increasingly meaningful as the Church has become conscious of its fragmented condition and concerned to find a basis for unity. This phrase, in the words of a distinguished churchman, means that Christ is not a ghost; he has a body, the Church. And it means that the Church is not a corpse; it has a spirit, Christ's.[4] We know from the Gospel record what things Christ did when he was on earth in his physical body. These are the things the Church should be doing today, for it is his body! The Church must speak the words and do the deeds that Christ would speak and do.

4. INDIVIDUAL CHRISTIANS, TO CONTINUE PAUL'S METAPHOR, ARE THE MEMBERS OF CHRIST'S BODY. They are the fingers, muscles, and cells that do his work. Just as the organs of the body do not all do the same work, but are all, no matter how humble, necessary to the functioning of the body, so every member is needed if the church is to function at its best. To refuse participation in the life of the church because you can be "just as good" without it is to remove your cell from its place in the body of Christ where it could draw strength and renewal from the body. It is also to limit by so much the effective-

---

[3] Harris Franklin Rall, *Together*, November, 1956, copyright © Pierce & Washabaugh.

[4] The late Dean Clarence Tucker Craig of Drew Theological Seminary in an address at an interseminary conference.

ness of the whole body. As C. S. Lewis has put it, "If you want to help those outside you must add your own little cell to the body of Christ who *can* help them. Cutting off a man's fingers would be an odd way of getting him to do more work." [5]

The conclusion of the matter is that to be Christian we do need the church—and the church needs us. There remains to ask in what ways the Christian relates himself to the life of the church.

III

FIRST OF ALL, THE CHRISTIAN WILL PARTICIPATE IN THE WORSHIP LIFE OF THE CHURCH. Earlier we have seen the importance of private worship, but this is not enough. Personal devotion needs the support and correction of the worship of the entire church. Furthermore, faithful, regular attendance at public worship offers us one way in which every Christian can witness to his faith. We do not all have the ability to make verbal testimony to others. We do not all have the financial means to make the gifts we might like to make. However, every Christian man, woman, and child can make the testimony to his neighbors of going to public worship and offering his prayer and praise unto God. By this simple act he acknowledges his dependence upon God, testifies to his love for Christ and the church, and seeks God's guidance for his life.

---

[5] *The Case for Christianity* (New York: The Macmillan Co., 1943), page 55. Used by permission of the publisher.

What participation in the worship life of the church can do for people who have been long removed from it, or perhaps have never known it, is movingly told by a young woman who writes of her struggle to be a mature and helpful wife.

Since we had moved to a strange city and Rob was taking his night courses, we had slid into the pattern of many young childless couples. Sunday we slept late, lazed over breakfast and newspapers, and dressed in sloppy clothes. Sunday bedtime had begun to leave me with a feeling of aimlessness framed in a resentment for the week ahead because my free day with Rob had ended.

Then one Sunday morning it occurred to me that we should vary the routine by going to church. Rob said, "Why not?" so we went. Again to sing familiar hymns, to sit quietly for an hour listening to out-reaching ideas, and to share that special companionship of reverence and worship—well, I felt as though I had tuned in on something greater than the love of Louise and Rob Evans. My mental house was in order and I was ready for the week ahead. . . .

As a child, Rob had had little religious training, had seldom attended any church. But he found new friends, some of them he had known in business, sitting in pews beside us. As we listened to sermons, then talked about them as we strolled home, he opened to me a side of his nature I had never seen before. We were drawn into a deeper relationship of understanding, and there was real joy for me

ON BEING A CHRISTIAN

in learning how our minds agreed on spiritual matters.[6]

One of the conspicuous failures of Protestantism has been in this area of public worship. *We have not taught our people that worship is a service they owe to God.* Consequently many church members attend services only on special days or when it is convenient, or when nothing else comes up. If they do not like the minister, or the music, or some lay leader in the church, they stay away. This is to equate the church with entertainment that we value for what it does for us. Actually, true worship may bring us pain, for when we sit in silence before God, we have a chance to see ourselves as we really are. As we hear the Scripture and listen to the sermon, we have God's ideal for human life held before us; and this may call upon us to make radical changes in our attitudes and practices. However, if we think of worship as a service we do for God, we are saved from seeking to impose our wills and our pleasure upon the church.

In part our difficulty is that we have not been taught how to worship. At this point Professor Nels Ferré has some helpful counsel:

Try preparing for church at home. Tuck the Sunday paper out of sight, play a hymn, read devotional literature, have a season of prayer. . . . Thus prepared, upon entering the sanctuary recall

[6] Louise Evans, "How to Help Your Husband." From *Together*, November, 1956, Copyright © Pierce & Washabaugh.

TO BE CHRISTIAN DO WE NEED THE CHURCH?

the purpose of coming to church. Identify yourself with the members of the congregation and their common seeking. Enter into the hopes of the minister and choir. As you sit or kneel, open your life in prayer that you be delivered from all defensiveness, ready to receive, and willing to do as well as to hear the truth. As the service proceeds join in each act, thanking God for the people participating and lifting up the whole congregation to God in order that its needs be met and its talents be used to help the world in all its confusion, despair and danger. Offer yourself and the people with the offering and trust God insistently for the result. If the service includes preaching, pray for the minister. Keep expecting great and real things to happen. The fruit may seem intangible and incapable of proof; but it will be real and good.[7]

IV

TO BE CHRISTIAN WE MUST PARTICIPATE IN THE CHURCH'S EFFORT TO PRESENT THE CLAIMS OF CHRIST TO THE UN-CHURCHED. In America, where the culture has been deeply influenced by Christianity so that the differences between the Christian and the non-Christian have become obscured, it is hard to realize that only a minority of the world's people are Christians. However, the world around, only three out of every ten persons belong to Christian churches. In England it is estimated that only 10 to 15 per cent of the population is closely

[7] *Op. cit.*, page 83. Used by permission of Harper & Bros.

linked to some church, while 25 to 30 per cent is sufficiently interested to attend church on great occasions, and 45 to 50 per cent is indifferent to religion.[8] Even in the United States, where since World War II and Korea there has been heightened interest in religion, only 61 per cent of the population claim membership in any church, and many of these have only marginal commitment. If the national average prevails in your community, four out of ten people you meet are unchurched!

WHAT IS THE CHRISTIAN'S RESONSIBILITY FOR THOSE OUTSIDE THE COMMUNITY OF FAITH? In an earlier day the conviction that all who had not found salvation in Christ would be eternally damned motivated earnest Christians to intense evangelistic effort. In these softer days the idea is widely held that God could not be guilty of cruelty that men would shrink from, and after all, if a man lives decently, is good to his family and generous to the community fund, will God turn his back on him? This viewpoint is particularly subversive to missionary effort when applied to members of other world religions. Are not all the great faiths, it is asked, simply roads up different sides of the same mountain? Indeed, some go so far as to insist that the exclusive claims of Christianity constitute a major obstacle to world unity and understanding.

This modern mood presents the thoughtful Christian with a dual challenge. *Is the revelation of God which*

---

[8] *Toward the Conversion of England,* report of the Archbishops' Commission on Evangelism, 1945, page 3, footnote.

132

Christian faith sees in Christ unique? And do people get along just as well without Christianity as with it?

As to the first question, it was faced nineteen centuries ago by the great apostle to the pagan Greco-Roman world. Paul told the people of Lystra that God had not left himself without witness in any generation (Acts 14:15-17), but he declared in Athens that "the times of ignorance God overlooked, but now he commands all men everywhere to repent, because he has fixed a day on which he will judge the world in righteousness by a man whom he has appointed" (Acts 17:30-31*a* R.S.V.). Christians regard other religions as preparing the way for Christ. (Paul called Judaism a "schoolmaster"— translated "custodian" in the Revised Standard Version— to bring us to Christ.) They find in them much that is harmonious with Christian teaching, but they see nothing in any other religion which alters the judgment that in a unique sense Christ is the Word made flesh, *"the* way, *the* truth, and *the* life."

AND WHAT OF THE VIEW THAT PEOPLE GET ALONG ALL RIGHT WITHOUT CHRIST? You do not have to observe the superstition and fetish worship of primitive tribes to answer that question. You do not have to see India's caste system in operation or atheistic Russia's disregard of human life. You know people in your own community and in your own circle of acquaintance who have not made Christ the Lord of their lives. How do they get along?

Consider first how much these persons may be living by Christian attitudes and standards ingrained in childhood or unconsciously absorbed from the culture. *Many of today's "decent, godless people" run on spiritual batteries charged by earlier generations.* Also look beneath the surface veneer of "success" and gaiety. Really how are people making out who try to live without the God who comes to us in Christ? What supports them in times of personal crisis and tragedy? What ground do they have for believing that goodness, generosity, and truth will prevail? What basis is there for any behavior not dictated by selfishness and greed? A poet has called ours the Age of Anxiety. A novelist writes of *Darkness at Noon.* One of our greatest dramatists called his last play *Long Day's Journey Into Night.* The characters in all these contemporary works are represented as men and women without faith, searching desperately for something to live by and die for. *Is anyone really getting along all right without Christian faith?*

The unchurched and uncommitted confront us on every hand. *To be a Christian means at least that we show concern for these persons for whom Christ died.* A young minister located more than fifty families in his parish who were of Protestant background but belonged to no church. When he challenged his church board to visit and interest these people, he was told: "They know the church is here. If they want it, let them come." To be sure, we do not all have the same gifts. Not all can preach and do pastoral work. Some will make the witness of gracious, victorious personal living. Others will lead or participate in visitation on behalf of the church and church school. But few there be who cannot practice

134

the evangelism of Philip: "Come and see." Concern for and effort to win the non-Christian is part of the vocation of the church.

V

TO BE CHRISTIAN WE ALSO NEED TO PARTICIPATE IN THE CHURCH'S PROGRAM OF COMMUNITY AND WORLD SERVICE. The famed historian Arnold Toynbee has told us that to live together as brothers is the only future the world has. One needs only to read the latest paper or listen to the next newscast to learn how far short of living as brothers we are. On the community level there are juvenile delinquency, political corruption, conflict between racial and economic groups, inequality of opportunity, and indifference to the lot of the less fortunate. On the world front there are a ruthless struggle for power, exploitation of colonial peoples and underdeveloped areas, a determined defense of their position by the "have" nations and a dynamic struggle for improvement by the "have nots."

A Christian who has learned to look upon his fellow men with the compassion of Christ will see them as neighbors whom he loves as he loves himself. HE WILL WISH TO BE A MEDIUM THROUGH WHICH GOD'S WILL IN THE WORLD CAN BE DONE. But what can he do to implement his good will? As an individual he is only one against entrenched and powerful forces of evil. He can—and should—join a political party and work for candidates and policies he feels move in the direction of "the greatest good for the greatest number." However, he will be naïve indeed if he does not know that *all political action involves compromise and that laws only provide social controls—they do not change hearts and wills.* Membership in labor unions, employers' associations, civic groups, and societies to promote every conceivable good cause will be open to the Christian. He should participate in such of these as his situation, time, and means allow. But he will soon discover that the membership of these groups do not all share the Christian ideal and that many of them seek special advantage rather than the common good.

Just as he is about to become disheartened about the possibility of doing anything to move the world toward brotherhood, the Christian may well remember the church and ask whether he has really related himself to it in a creative way. *The church, changing people from selfishness to unselfishness, from indifference to concern, is doing the quiet basic work needed to create a new society.* To be sure, in its local manifestation the church does not always look like a very promising medium for changing the world. All too often it is weak and divided. Its members, being human, are frequently absorbed in their own concerns and indifferent to events on the world horizon. Nevertheless the church is the body of Christ, the physical organism upon which he relies for the execution of his will. And the local congregation, by itself so inadequate, is only one cell of a great world-wide body.

It has been said that "the church is the conscience of society." Historically this has been true. With regard to the dignity and worth of the individual, the position of women, the exploitation of children for cheap labor, the institution of slavery, the ideal of sobriety—in all these and many others it has been the voice of the church that has created an awareness of the problem, a conviction of wrongdoing, and finally a new and better ordering of life. Currently it is still the church that must serve as the conscience of civilization in regard to the status of colonial peoples, the taming of atomic energy, the ending of racial discrimination, and the establishment of international order. *If the church is to be an effective voice for the Christian conscience, the individual Christian must place himself in such relation to the church that he can first hear its correction to his own attitudes and then support its witness to society at large.*

BUT THE CHURCH DOES MORE THAN SPEAK. IT ALSO ACTS. One pastor has become concerned about the increasing slaughter upon the highways and is leading his people to find ways in which they can apply the commandment "Thou shalt not kill" to this area. Another church has led its community to provide more adequate recreation facilities for its young people as an answer to juvenile misdemeanors. A church federation has alerted its community to the vicious and pornographic publications displayed on its newsstands. Many pastors and churches have served as mediating influences in areas of racial tension and threatened conflict. Often the church can provide a meeting place for such organizations as Alcoholics Anonymous which reach and serve persons the church cannot ordinarily contact. Of course one could enumerate indefinitely the community services of the church through its hospitals, homes, community and social centers, its home mission schools, its colleges and universities, and so on. The church offers the concerned person a way to relate himself to all these and other programs for lifting the community and nation closer to the Christian ideal.

THE CHURCH ALSO OFFERS A PROGRAM FOR WINNING THE WORLD TO THE CHRISTIAN IDEAL—THE CHRISTIAN MISSIONARY ENTERPRISE. The nineteenth century and the twentieth up to World War II saw the gospel carried to every land and preached in every language. By September, 1939, devoted missionaries had established work in six thousand centers in one hundred countries. Although a tiny minority, nevertheless these churches constituted islands of love and concern which with the home churches made up a world Christian community. Even in the midst of war tenuous contacts were maintained. Many missionaries chose to stay at their posts even when this meant years of internment and privation.

Since the war the tide of expansion has been halted. In Communist-dominated countries every obstacle is placed in the way of Christian work. All foreign leadership has been expelled from China, and the national leaders have been isolated from contact with the world church. In other lands the rising tide of nationalism has made missionary activity increasingly difficult. Unfortunately Christianity has been so identified in many minds with the policies of colonial powers that Western connections are a handicap and even native Christians are suspect. A century which began with a heroic determination to "win the world for Christ in this generation" came to its halfway point with missions on the defensive on most fronts.

YET THE WINNING OF THE WORLD AND ITS PEOPLE TO COMMON LOYALTY TO CHRIST REMAINS THE WORLD'S "LAST, BEST HOPE" TO FIND A COMMON BASIS OF UNITY. Can the faithful congregations of Chinese Christians hold out until communication is re-established with the outside world? Can Christianity, hampered by the *apartheid* policies of Christian South Africa, win the battle for Africa against Islam and Communism, which boast of no racial discrimination? Can Indian Christians survive the anti-British and anti-Western spirit in that land? No man of good will who longs for the establishment of world order based on justice can be indifferent to the progress of Christian missions. Participation in that mission with informed and sacrificial effort is part of what it means to be a Christian.

FOR THOUGHT AND DISCUSSION

Biblical background: Read the account of the birthday of the Church in Acts 2. Compare the origin of the Christian Church with the Constitutional Convention which originated the structure of our government.

Read I Corinthians 12:12-27; Ephesians 4:11-16. What does the New Testament mean by calling the Church "the body of Christ"? Does this figure of speech give you a new understanding of the Church? In what way?

How would you explain this concept to a new Christian convert from another faith?

How would you meet the argument, "I don't need the church in order to be a Christian"?

What is the difference between a fellowship of believers and other kinds of fellowships? Are all fellowships of believers churches? What makes a fellowship a Christian church?

Why is regular attendance at public worship important for the Christian life?

How does the church perform its function as "the conscience of society"? Illustrate in terms of one or more issues of current public concern.

In what ways is your church active in making your community a more Christian place to live? Are there other things you should be doing? How can the individual Christian participate in these efforts?

In what ways is your church related to efforts to win the world to Christian loyalty? If you were asked to debate the affirmative of the proposition, "Resolved: that Christian missions are a more hopeful program for world unity than the United Nations," how would you present your case?